Gramley Library
Salem College
Winston-Salem, NC 27108

SELECTED POEMS

Books by John Gould Fletcher

FIRE AND WINE

IRRADIATIONS—SAND AND SPRAY

GOBLINS AND PAGODAS

JAPANESE PRINTS

THE TREE OF LIFE

BREAKERS AND GRANITE

PAUL GAUGUIN, HIS LIFE AND ART

PRELUDES AND SYMPHONIES

PARABLES

BRANCHES OF ADAM

JOHN SMITH—ALSO POCAHONTAS

THE BLACK ROCK

THE TWO FRONTIERS

XXIV ELEGIES

LIFE IS MY SONG

SELECTED POEMS

(Translator)

THE DANCE OVER FIRE AND WATER

THE REVERIES OF A SOLITARY

SELECTED POEMS

by

JOHN GOULD FLETCHER

WITHDRAWN

FARRAR & RINEHART, INC.

NEW YORK   TORONTO

SALEM COLLEGE LIBRARY
Winston-Salem, North Carolina

COPYRIGHT, 1938, BY JOHN GOULD FLETCHER
PRINTED IN THE UNITED STATES OF AMERICA

ALL RIGHTS RESERVED

To

CHARLIE MAY

THIS, AND ALL MY FUTURE BOOKS

21637

ACKNOWLEDGMENT

This volume of selections from my work, covering the years from 1913 to the present, has been taken from the following books: IRRADIATIONS—SAND AND SPRAY, published by Houghton Mifflin in 1915; GOBLINS AND PAGODAS, published by the same firm in 1916; THE TREE OF LIFE, published by Chatto and Windus of London, in 1918; BREAKERS AND GRANITE, published by The Macmillan Company in 1921; THE BLACK ROCK, published by Faber of London, in 1928; PRELUDES AND SYMPHONIES, published by The Macmillan Company in 1930, and XXIV ELEGIES, published by Writers' Editions of Santa Fé, New Mexico, in 1935.

Grateful acknowledgment is hereby made to these publishers for permission to reprint what I wish to be saved from these volumes.

CONTENTS

PART ONE

PART TWO

PART THREE

[x]

SALEM COLLEGE LIBRARY
Winston-Salem, North Carolina

PART ONE

IRRADIATIONS

I

The spattering of the rain upon pale terraces
Of afternoon is like the passing of a dream
Amid the roses shuddering 'gainst the wet green stalks
Of the streaming trees—the passing of the wind
Upon the pale lower terraces of my dream
Is like the crinkling of the wet grey robes
Of the hours that come to turn over the urn
Of the day and spill its rainy dream.
Vague movement over the puddled terraces:
Heavy gold pennons—a pomp of solemn gardens
Half hidden under the liquid veil of spring:
Far trumpets like a vague rout of faded roses
Burst 'gainst the wet green silence of distant forests:
A clash of cymbals—then the swift swaying footsteps
Of the wind that undulates along the languid terraces.
Pools of rain—the vacant terraces
Wet, chill and glistening
Towards the sunset beyond the broken doors of to-day.

In the grey skirts of the fog seamews skirl desolately,
And flick like bits of paper propelled by a wind
About the flabby sails of a departing ship
Crawling slowly down the low reaches
Of the river.
About the keel there is a bubbling and gurgling
Of grumpy water;
And as the prow noses out a way for itself,
It seems to weave a dream of bubbles and flashing foam,
A dream of strange islands whereto it is bound:
Pearl-islands drenched with the dawn.
The palms flash under the immense dark sky,
Down which the sun dives to embrace the earth:
Drums boom and conches bray,
And with a crash of crimson cymbals
Suddenly appears above the polished backs of slaves
A king in a breastplate of gold
Gigantic
Amid tossed roses and swaying dancers
That melt into pale undulations and muffled echoes
'Mid the bubbling of the muddy lumpy water,
And the swirling of the seamews above the sullen river.

III

Over the roof-tops race the shadows of clouds;
Like horses the shadows of clouds charge down the street.

Whirlpools of purple and gold,
Winds from the mountains of cinnabar,
Lacquered mandarin moments, palanquins swaying and balancing
Amid the vermilion pavilions, against the jade balustrades.
Glint of the glittering wings of dragon-flies in the light:
Silver filaments, golden flakes settling downwards,
Rippling, quivering flutters, repulse and surrender,
The sun broidered upon the rain,
The rain rustling with the sun.

Over the roof-tops race the shadows of clouds;
Like horses the shadows of clouds charge down the street.

IV

Flickering of incessant rain
On flashing pavements:
Sudden scurry of umbrellas:
Bending, recurved blossoms of the storm.

The winds come clanging and clattering
From long white highroads whipping in ribbons up summits:
They strew upon the city gusty wafts of apple-blossom,
And the rustling of innumerable translucent leaves.

Uneven, tinkling, the lazy rain
Dripping from the eaves.

V

The houses of the city no longer hum and play:
They lie like careless drowsy giants, dumb, estranged.

One presses to his breast his toy, a lighted pane:
One stirs uneasily: one is cold in death.

And the late moon, fearfully peering over an immense
  shoulder,
Sees, in the shadow below, the unpeopled hush of a street.

VI

O seeded grass, you army of little men
Crawling up the long slope with quivering, quick blades of
  steel:
You who storm millions of graves, tiny green tentacles of
  earth,
Interlace yourselves tightly over my heart,
And do not let me go:
For I would lie here forever and watch with one eye
The pilgrimaging ants in your dull, savage jungles,
The while with the other I see the stiff lines of the slope
Break in mid-air, a wave surprisingly arrested;
And above it, wavering, dancing, bodiless, colourless, unreal,
The long thin lazy fingers of the heat.

An ant crawling up a grass-blade,
And above it, the sky.
I shall remember these when I die:
An ant and a butterfly
And the sky.

The grass is full of forget-me-nots and poppies:
Through the air darts many a fly.
The ant toils up its grass-blade,
The careless hours go by.

The grass-blades bow to the feet of the lazy hours:
They walk out of the wood, showering shadows on flowers.
Their robes flutter vaguely far off there in the clearing:
I see them sometimes from the corner of my eye.

VIII

The morning is clean and blue and the wind blows up the
    clouds.
Now my thoughts gathered from afar
Once again in their patched armour, with rusty plumes and
    blunted swords,
Move out to war.

Smoking our morning pipes we shall ride two and two
Through the woods.
For our old cause keeps us together,
And our hatred is so precious not death or defeat can break
    it.

[7]

God willing, we shall this day meet that old enemy
Who has given us so many a good beating.
Thank God we have a cause worth fighting for,
And a cause worth losing and a good song to sing.

IX

All you stars up yonder,
Do you hear me? Beautiful, winking, sullen eyes,
I am tired of seeing you in the same old places,
Night after night in the sky.
I hoped you would dance—but after twenty-six years,
I find you are determined to stay as you are.
So I make it known to you, stars clustered or solitary,
That I want you to fall into my lap to-night.
Come down, little stars, let me play with you:
I will string you like beads, and shovel you together,
And wear you in my ears, and scatter you over people—
And toss you back, like apples, if I choose.

X

Slowly along the lamp-emblazoned street,
Amid the last sad drifting crowds of midnight,
Like lost souls wandering,
Comes marching by solemnly
As for some gem-bedecked ritual of old,
A monotonous procession of black carts
Full crowded with blood-red blossom:
Scarlet geraniums

[8]

Unfolding their fiery globes upon the night.
These are the memories of day moulded in jagged flame:
Lust, joy, blood, and death.
With crushed hands, weary eyes, and hoarse clamor,
We consecrate and acclaim them tumultuously,
Ere they pass, contemptuous, beyond the unpierced veil of
    silence.

XI

I think there was an hour in which God laughed at me,
For as I passed along the street,
I saw that all the women—although their bodies were dex-
    terously concealed—
Were thinking with all their might what the men were like:
And the men, mechanically correct, cigars at lips,
Were wanting to rush at the women,
But were restrained by respectability or timidity,
Or fear of the consequences or vanity or some puerile dream
Of a pale ideal lost in the vast grey sky.
So I said to myself, it is time to end all this:
I will take the first woman that comes along.
And then God laughed at me—and I too smiled
To see that He was in such good humour and that the sun
    was shining.

XII

It is evening, and the earth
Wraps her shoulders in an old blue shawl.
Afar off there clink the polychrome points of the stars,
Indefatigable, after all these years!

Here upon earth there is life, and then death,
Dawn, and later nightfall,
Fire, and the quenching of embers:
But why should I not remember that my night is dawn in
    another part of the world,
If the idea fits my fancy?
Dawns of marvellous light, wakeful, sleepy, weary, dancing
    dawns,
You are rose petals settling through the blue of my evening:
I light my pipe to salute you,
And sit puffing smoke in the air and never say a word.

SAND AND SPRAY

THE GALE

Allegro furioso.

Pale green-white, in a gallop across the sky,
The clouds retreating from a perilous affray
Carry the moon with them, a heavy sack of gold;
Sharp arrows, stars between them shoot and play.

The wind, as it strikes the sands,
Clutches with rigid hands
And tears from them
Thin ribbons of pallid sleet,
Long, stinging, hissing drift,
Which it trails up inland.

I lean against the bitter wind:
My body plunges like a ship.

[10]

Out there I see grey breakers rise,
Their ravelled beards are white,
And foam is in their eyes.
My heart is blown from me to-night
To be transfixed by all the stars.

Steadily the wind
Rages up the shore:
In the trees it roars and battles,
With rattling drums
And heavy spears,
Towards the house-fronts on it comes.

The village, a loose mass outflung,
Breaks its path.
Between the walls
It bounces, tosses in its wrath.
It is broken, it is lost.

With green-grey eyes,
With whirling arms,
With clashing feet,
With bellowing lungs,
Pale green-white in a gallop across the sky,
The wind comes.

The great gale of the winter flings himself flat upon earth.

He hurriedly scribbles on the sand
His transient tragic destiny.

[11]

SALEM COLLEGE LIBRARY
Winston-Salem, North Carolina

THE TIDE

The tide makes music
At the foot of the beach;
The waves sing together,
Rumble of breakers.
Ships there are swaying
Into the distance,
Thrum of the cordage,
Slap of the sails.

The tide makes music
At the foot of the beach;
Low notes of an organ
'Gainst the dull clang of bells.
The tide's tense purple
On the untrodden sand:
Its throat is blue,
Its hands are gold.

The tide makes music:
The tide all day
Catches light from the clouds
That float over the sky.
Ocean, old serpent,
Coils up and uncoils;
With sinuous motion,
With rustle of scales.

Maestoso.

Like black plunging dolphins with red bellies,
The steamers in herds
Swim through the choppy breakers
On this day of winds and clouds.
Wallowing and plunging,
They seek their path,
The smoke of their snorting
Hangs in the sky.

Like black plunging dolphins with red bellies,
The steamers pass,
Flapping their propellers
Salt with the spray.
Their iron sides glisten,
Their stays thrash:
Their funnels quiver
With the heat from beneath.

Like black plunging dolphins with red bellies,
The steamers together
Dive and roll through the tumult
Of green hissing water.
These are the avid of spoil,
Gleaners of the seas,
They loom on their adventure
Up purple and chrome horizons.

[13]

THE NIGHT WIND

Adagio lamentoso.

Wind of the night, wind of the long cool shadows,
Wind from the garden gate stealing up the avenue,
Wind caressing my cool pale cheek completely,
All my happiness goes out to you.

Wind flapping aimlessly at my yellow window curtain,
Wind suddenly insisting on your way down to the sea,
Buoyant wind, sobbing wind, wind shuddering and plaintive,
Why do you come from beyond through the night's blue
     mystery?

Wind of my dream, wind of the delicate beauty,
Wind strumming idly at the harp-strings of my heart:
Wind of the autumn—O melancholy beauty,
Touch me once—one instant—you and I shall never part!

Wind of the night, wind that has fallen silent,
Wind from the dark beyond crying suddenly, eerily,
What terrible news have you shrieked out there in the still-
    ness?
The night is cool and quiet and the wind has crept to sea.

TIDE OF STORMS

Allegro con fuoco.

Crooked, crawling tide with long wet fingers
Clutching at the gritty beach in the roar and spurt of spray,
Tide of gales, drunken tide, lava-burst of breakers,
Black ships plunge upon you from sea to sea away.

[14]

Shattering tide, tide of winds, tide of the long still winter,
What matter though ships fail, men sink, there vanish glory?
War-clouds shall hurl their stinging sleet upon our last ad-
    venture,
Night-winds shall brokenly whisper our bitter, tragic story.

BLUE SYMPHONY

I

The darkness rolls upward.
The thick darkness carries with it
Rain and a ravel of cloud.
The sun comes forth upon earth.

Palely the dawn
Leaves me facing timidly
Old gardens sunken:
And in the walks is water.

Sombre wreck—autumnal leaves;
Shadowy roofs
In the blue mist,
And a willow-branch that is broken.

Oh, old pagodas of my soul, how you glittered across green
    trees!

Blue and cool:
Blue, tremulously,
Blow faint puffs of smoke
Across sombre pools.
The damp green smell of rotted wood;
And a heron that cries from out the water.

II

Through the upland meadows
I go alone.
For I dreamed of someone last night
Who is waiting for me.

Flower and blossom, tell me, do you know of her?

Have the rocks hidden her voice?
They are very blue and still.

Long upward road that is leading me,
Light-hearted I quit you,
For the long loose ripples of the meadow-grass
Invite me to dance upon them.

Quivering grass
Daintily poised
For her foot's tripping.

Oh, blown clouds, could I only race up like you,
Oh, the last slopes that are sun-drenched and steep!

Look, the sky!
Across black valleys
Rise blue-white aloft
Jaggéd unwrinkled mountains, ranges of death.

Solitude. Silence.

III

One chuckles by the brook for me:
One rages under the stone.
One makes a spout of his mouth;
One whispers—one is gone.

One over there on the water
Spreads cold ripples
For me
Enticingly.

The vast dark trees
Flow like blue veils
Of tears
Into the water.

Sour sprites,
Moaning and chuckling,
What have you hidden from me?

"In the palace of the blue stone she lies forever
Bound hand and foot."

[17]

Was it the wind
That rattled the reeds together?

Dry reeds,
A faint shiver in the grasses.

IV

On the left hand there is a temple:
And a palace on the right-hand side.
Foot-passengers in scarlet
Pass over the glittering tide.

Under the bridge
The old river flows
Low and monotonous
Day after day.

I have heard and have seen
All the news that has been:
Autumn's gold and Spring's green!

Now in my palace
I see foot-passengers
Crossing the river:
Pilgrims of autumn
In the afternoons.

Lotus pools:
Petals in the water.
These are my dreams.

For me silks are outspread.
I take my ease, unthinking.

v

And now the lowest pine-branch
Is drawn across the disk of the sun.
Old friends who will forget me soon,
I must go on
Towards those blue death-mountains
I have forgot so long.

In the marsh grasses
There lies forever
My last treasure,
With the hopes of my heart.

The ice is glazing over,
Torn lanterns flutter,
On the leaves is snow.

In the frosty evening
Toll the old bell for me,
Once, in the sleepy temple.

Perhaps my soul will hear.

Afterglow:
Before the stars peep
I shall creep out into darkness.

GREEN SYMPHONY

I

The glittering leaves of the rhododendrons
Balance and vibrate in the cool air;
While in the sky above them
White clouds chase each other.

Like scampering rabbits,
Flashes of sunlight sweep the lawn;
They fling in passing
Patterns of shadow,
Golden and green.

With long cascades of laughter,
The mating birds dart and swoop to the turf:
'Mid their mad trillings
Glints the gay sun behind the trees.

Down there are deep blue lakes:
Orange blossom droops in the water.

In the tower of the winds,
All the bells are set adrift:
Jingling
For the dawn.

Thin fluttering streamers
Of breeze lash through the swaying boughs;

Palely expectant
The earth receives the slanting rain.

I am a glittering raindrop
Hugged close by the cool rhododendron.
I am a daisy starring
The exquisite curves of the close-cropped turf.

The glittering leaves of the rhododendron
Are shaken like blue-green blades of grass,
Flickering, cracking, falling:
Splintering in a million fragments.

The wind runs laughing up the slope
Stripping off handfuls of wet green leaves,
To fling in people's faces.
Wallowing on the daisy-powdered turf,
Clutching at the sunlight,
Cavorting in the shadow.

Like baroque pearls,
Like cloudy emeralds,
The clouds and the trees clash together;
Whirling and swirling
In the tumult
Of the spring,
And the wind.

The trees splash the sky with their fingers,
A restless green rout of stars.

With whirling movement
They swing their boughs
About their stems:
Planes on planes of light and shadow
Pass among them,
Opening fanlike to fall.

The trees are like a sea;
Tossing,
Trembling,
Roaring,
Wallowing,
Darting their long green flickering fronds up at the sky,
Spotted with white blossom-spray.

The trees are roofs:
Hollow caverns of cool blue shadow,
Solemn arches
In the afternoons.
The whole vast horizon
In terrace beyond terrace,
Pinnacle above pinnacle,
Lifts to the sky
Serrated ranks of green on green.

They caress the roofs with their fingers,
They sprawl about the river to look into it;
Up the hill they come
Gesticulating challenge:
They cower together
In dark valleys;
They yearn out over the fields.

Enamelled domes
Tumble upon the grass,
Crashing in ruin
Quiet at last.

The trees lash the sky with their leaves,
Uneasily shaking their dark green manes.

III

Far let the voices of the mad wild birds be calling me,
I will abide in this forest of pines.

When the wind blows,
Battling through the forest,
I hear it distantly,
The crash of a perpetual sea.

When the rain falls,
I watch silver spears slanting downwards
From pale river-pools of sky,
Enclosed in dark fronds.

When the sun shines,
I weave together far branches till they shape mighty circles,
I sway to the movement of hooded summits,
I swim leisurely in deep blue seas of air.

I hug the smooth bark of stately red pillars,
And with cones carefully scattered
I mark the progression of dark dial-shadows
Flung diagonally downwards through the afternoon.

This turf is not like turf:
It is a smooth dry carpet of velvet,
Embroidered with brown patterns of needles and cones.
These trees are not like trees:
They are innumerable feathery pagoda-umbrellas,
Stiffly ungracious to the wind,
Teetering on red-lacquered stems.

In the evening I listen to the winds' lisping,
While the conflagrations of the sunset flicker and clash be-
        hind me,
Flamboyant crenellations of glory amid the charred ebony
        boles.

In the night the fiery nightingales
Shall clash and trill through the silence:
Like the voices of mermaids crying
From the sea.

Long ago has the moon whelmed this uncompleted temple.
Stars swim like gold fish far above the black arches.

Far let the timid feet of dawn fly to catch me:
I will abide in this forest of pines:
For I have unveiled naked beauty,
And the things that she whispered to me in the darkness
Are buried deep in my heart.

Now let the black tops of the pine-trees break like a spent
    wave,
Against the grey sky:
These are tombs and memorials and temples and altars sun-
    kindled for me.

WHITE SYMPHONY

I

Forlorn and white,
Whorls of purity about a golden chalice,
Immense the peonies
Flare and shatter their petals over my face.

They slowly turn paler,
They seem to be melting like blue-grey flakes of ice,
Thin greyish shivers
Fluctuating 'mid the dark green lance-thrust of the leaves.

Like snowballs tossed,
Like soft white butterflies,
The peonies poise in the twilight.
And their narcotic insinuating perfume

Draws me into them,
Shivering with the coolness,
Aching with the void.
They kiss the blue chalice of my dreams
Like a gesture seen for an instant and then lost forever.

Outwards the petals
Thrust to embrace me,
Pale daggers of coldness
Run through my aching breast.

Outwards, still outwards,
Till on the brink of twilight
They swirl downwards silently,
Flurry of snow in the void.

Outwards, still outwards,
Till the blue walls are hidden,
And in the blinding white radiance
Of a whirlpool of clouds, I awake.

Like spraying rockets
My peonies shower
Their glories on the night.

Wavering perfumes,
Drift about the garden;
Shadows of the moonlight,
Drift and ripple over the dew-gemmed leaves.

Soar, crash, and sparkle,
Shoal of stars drifting
Like silver fishes,
Through the black sluggish boughs.

Towards the impossible,
Towards the inaccessible,
Towards the ultimate,
Towards the silence,
Towards the eternal,
These blossoms go.

The peonies spring like rockets in the twilight,
And out of them all I rise.

II

Downwards through the blue abyss it slides,
The white snow-water of my dreams,
Downwards crashing from slippery rock
Into the boiling chasm:
In which no eye dare look, for it is the chasm of death.

Upwards from the blue abyss it rises,
The chill water-mist of my dreams;
Upwards to greyish weeping pines,
And to skies of autumn ever about my heart,
It is blue at the beginning,
And blue-white against the grey-greenness;
It wavers in the upper air,

[27]

Catching unconscious sparkles, a rainbow-glint of sunlight,
And fading in the sad depths of the sky.

Outwards rush the strong pale clouds,
Outwards and ever outwards;
The blue-grey clouds indistinguishable one from another:
Nervous, sinewy, tossing their arms and brandishing,
Till on the blue serrations of the horizon
They drench with their black rain a great peak of changeless
  snow.

As evening came on, I climbed the tower,
To gaze upon the city far beneath:
I was not weary of day; but in the evening
A white mist assembled and gathered over the earth
And blotted it from sight.

But to escape:
To chase with the golden clouds galloping over the horizon:
Arrows of the northwest wind
Singing amid them,
Ruffling up my hair!

As evening came on the distance altered;
Pale wavering reflections rose from out the city,
Like sighs or the beckoning of half-visible hands.
Monotonously and sluggishly they crept upwards,
A river that had spent itself in some chasm,
And dwindled and foamed at last at my weary feet.

Autumn! Golden fountains,
And the winds neighing
Amid the monotonous hills:
Desolation of the old gods,
Rain that lifts and rain that moves away;
In the green-black torrent
Scarlet leaves.

It was now perfectly evening:
And the tower loomed like a gaunt peak in mid-air
Above the city: its base was utterly lost.
It was slowly coming on to rain,
And the immense columns of white mist
Wavered and broke before the faint-hurled spears.

I will descend the mountains like a shepherd,
And in the folds of tumultuous misty cities,
I will put all my thoughts, all my old thoughts, safely to
    sleep.
For it is already autumn,
O whiteness of the pale southwestern sky!
O wavering dream that was not mine to keep!

In midnight, in mournful moonlight,
By paths I could not trace,
I walked in the white garden,
Each flower had a white face.

Their perfume intoxicated me: thus I began my dream.

[29]

I was alone; I had no one to guide me,
But the moon was like the sun:
It stooped and kissed each waxen petal,
One after one.

Green and white was that garden: diamond rain hung in the
        branches,
You will not believe it!

In the morning, at the dayspring,
I wakened, shivering; lo,
The white garden that blossomed at my feet
Was a garden hidden in snow.

It was my sorrow to see that all this was a dream.

III

Blue, clogged with purple,
Mists uncoil themselves:
Sparkling to the horizon,
I see the snow alone.

In the deep blue chasm
Boats sleep under gold thatch;
Icicle-like trees fret
Faintly rose-touched sky.

Under their heaped snow-eaves
Leaden houses shiver.

Through thin blue crevasses
Trickles an icy stream.

The pines groan, white-laden,
The waves shiver, struck by the wind;
Beyond from treeless horizons,
Broken snow-peaks crawl to the sea.

Wearily the snow glares,
Through the grey silence, day after day,
Mocking the colourless cloudless sky
With the reflection of death.

There is no smoke through the pine tops,
No strong red boatmen in pale green reeds,
No herons to flicker an instant,
No lanterns to glow with gay ray.

No sails beat up to the harbour,
With creaking cordage and sailors' song.
Somnolent, bare-poled, indifferent,
They sleep, and the city sleeps.

Mid-winter about them casts
Its dreary fortifications:
Each day is a gaunt grey rock,
And death is the last of them all.

Over the sluggish snow,
Drifts now a pallid weak shower of bloom;
Boredom of fresh creation,
Death-weariness of old returns.

White, white blossom,
Fall of the shattered cups day on day:
Is there anything here that is not ancient,
That has not bloomed a thousand years ago?

Under the glare of the white-hot day,
Under the restless wind-rakes of the winter,
White blossom or white snow scattered,
And beneath them, dark, the graves.

Dark graves never changing,
White dream drifting, never changing above them:
O that the white scroll of heaven might be rolled up,
And the naked red lightning thrust at the smouldering
    earth!

POPPIES OF THE RED YEAR

A SYMPHONY IN SCARLET

I

The words that I have written
To me become as poppies:
Deep angry disks of scarlet flame full-glowing in the stillness
Of a shut room.

Silken their edges undulate out to me,
Drooping on their hairy stems;
Flaring like folded shawls, down-curved like rockets starting
To break and shatter their light.

Wide-flaunting and heavy, crinkle-lipped blossom,
Darting faint shivers through me;
Globed Chinese lanterns on green silk cords a-swaying
Over motionless pools.

These are lamps of a festival of sleep held each night to
        welcome me,
Crimson-bursting through dark doors.
Out to the dull, blue, heavy fumes of opium rolling
From their rent red hearts, I go to seek my dream.

II

A riven wall like a face half torn away
Stares blankly at the evening:
And from a window like a crooked mouth
It barks at the sunset sky.

Out over there, beyond,
On plains where night has settled
Tent-like encampments of vaporous blue smoke or mist,
Three men are riding.

One of them looks and sees the sky:
One of them looks and sees the earth:

[33]

The last one looks and sees nothing at all.
They ride on.

One of them pauses and says, "It is death."
Another pauses and says, "It is life."
The last one pauses and says, " 'Tis a dream."
His bridle shakes.

The sky
Is filled with oval violet-tinted clouds
Through which the sun long settled strikes at random,
Enkindling here and there blotched circles of rosy light.

These are poppies,
Unclosing immense corollas,
Waving the horsemen on.

Over the earth, upheaving, folding,
They ride: their bridles shake:
One of them sees the sky is red:
One of them sees the earth is dark:
The last man sees he rides to his death,
Yet he says nothing at all.

III

There will be no harvest at all this year;
For the gaunt black slopes arising
Lift the wrinkled aching furrows of their fields, falling away,
To the rainy sky in vain.

But in the furrows
There is grass and many flowers.
Scarlet tossing poppies
Flutter their wind-slashed edges,
On which gorged black flies poise and sway in drunken sleep.

The black flies hang
Above the tangled, trampled grasses,
Grey, crumpled bundles lie in them:
They sprawl,
Heave faintly;
And between their stiffened fingers,
Run out clogged crimson trickles,
Spattering the poppies and standing in beads on the grass.

IV

I saw last night
Sudden puffs of flame in the northern sky.

The sky was an even expanse of rolling grey smoke,
Lit faintly by the moon that hung
Its white face in a dead tree to the east.

Within the depths of greenish, greyish smoke
Were roars,
Crackles and spheres of vapor,
And then
Huge disks of crimson shooting up, falling away.

And I said these are flower petals,
Sleep petals, dream petals,
Blown by the winds of a dream.

But still the crimson rockets rose.
They seemed to be
One great field of immense poppies burning evenly,
Casting their viscid perfume to the earth.

The earth is sown with dead,
And out of these the red
Blooms are pushing up, advancing higher,
And each night brings them nigher,
Closer, closer to my heart.

                    v

By the sluggish canal
That winds between thin ugly dunes,
There are no passing boats with creaking ropes to-day.

But when the evening
Crouches down, like a hurt rabbit,
Under the everlasting raincloud whirling up the north ho-
    rizon,
Downwards on the stream will float
Glowing points of fire.

Orange, coppery, scarlet,
Crimson, rosy, flickering,

They pass, the lanterns
Of the unknown dead.

Out where the sea, sailless,
Is mouthing and fretting
Its chaos of pebbles and dried sticks by the dunes.

By the wall of that house
That looks like a face half torn away,
And from its flat mouth barks at the sky,
The sky which is shot with broad red disks of light,
Petals drowsily falling.

VI

"It was not for a sacred cause,
Nor for faith, nor for new generations,
That unburied we roll and float
Beneath this flaming tumult of drunken sleep-flowers.

"But it was for a mad adventure,
Something we longed for, poisonous, seductive,
That we dared go out in the night together,
Towards the glow that called us,
On the unsown fields of death.

"Now we lie here reaped, ungarnered,
Red swaths of a new harvest:
But you who follow after,
Must struggle with our dream:

[37]

And out of its restless and oppressive night,
Filled with blue fumes, dull, choking,
You will draw hints of that vision
Which we hold aloof in silence."

PART TWO

THE WALK ON THE BEACH

The evening, blue, voluptuous, of June
Settled slowly on the beach with pulsating wings,
Like a sea-gull come to rest: far, far off twinkled
Gold lights from the towers of a city and a passing ship.
The dark sea rolled its body at the end of the beach,
The warm soft beach which it was too tired to climb,
And we two walked together there
Arm in arm, having nothing in our souls but love.

Your face shaded by the hat looked up at me;
Your pale face framed in the dark gold of your hair,
Your face with its dumb unforgettable look in the eyes,
A look I have only once seen, that I shall see never again.
Our steps were lost on the long vast carpet of sand,
Our souls were lost in the sky where the stars came out;
Our bodies clung together: time was not.
Love came and passed: our lives were cleaned and changed.

The winter will spill upon us soon its dark cruse laden with
    rain,
Time has broken our moorings; we have drifted apart; love
    is done.
I can only dream in the long still nights that we rest heart
    to heart,

I can only wake to the knowledge that my love is lost and
   won.
We were as two weak swallows, together to southward set,
Blown apart, vainly crying to each other while at strife with
   the seas.
We go out in the darkness; we speak but in memories;
But I have never forgotten and I shall never forget.

THE WALK IN THE GARDEN

Still and windless was the day,
The great green trees dreamed and gloomed
And drooped over each alleyway
Silent cascades of weary leaves;
They yellowed slowly,
Some of them blazed like orange suns.
The asters, violet and melancholy,
Would have dropt their petals had breezes come.

Aloft in the sky
Drowsily rode
Toppling peaks, autumnal cloud;
Cream-coloured snow dissolving
Into chill chasms of blue.
On through the sky
We watched them go,
How we wished we could climb their glistening sides
And rest on their summits together!

Hand in hand
We went all day,
For us was every flower a love-token;
Every tree a shower of jewels for you,
Every cloud a column of hope for me,
Every shadow a kiss,
Every sunbeam a joy,
And the sunlight flowed over and through us
Like a sea of golden dust washing two rocks
The sun threw over us
Carelessly his beauty.

You were I and I was you;
We were one together:
Wherever we went there was love for us,
Flowers and sunlight.
Yet there were spies and bonds on our love,
To snatch kisses from our hands,
To steal our joy,
In the melancholy splendor
Of the autumnal garden
Under the distant trees.

Still and windless was the day,
The great dark trees stood waiting;
Drooping their heavy-barked shoulders
Beneath the burden of yellow leaves.
In the afternoon a vast cloud rose,
And brandished his lightning-whip once over us:—
A flash and a clang,

[43]

While the rain's song hummed through the air.
The shower passed,
The west blazed as if it had received the kiss of darkness.

Then all too soon it grew to dusk;
Time was not—time and life were a dream—
A dream of the light that woke in your eyes,
A dream of the joy that sang in my heart;
A dream of the autumnal garden.
When the dusk came, our two souls flitted
Outwards for ever and ever together:
We did not heed the chill blue darkness,
For the night had no more power over us.

THE ASTER FLOWER

Pale on its stalk, the aster flower
Exhales its beauty to the night;
The dry leaves scatter on the grass,
Brown flecks on bits of jade.
The haze of autumn hides the trees,
To-night shall be turned the hour-glass of my life;
Now all my thoughts going homewards
In the distance are singing songs of you.

Purple and gold, the aster flower
Is an image of my autumnal love:
Its golden centre is like a torch
To kindle joy in the long still night,

A torch of love with violet rays,
Grief at its enigmatic heart:
Frail clustered flower of my dreams,
You shall bloom to-night, you shall bloom to-night.

The city is like an aster flower,
Out of the city I come to you,
Out of the purple heart of the night,
Swifter than song, lighter than light.
Purple and gold, my aster flower,
I am the wind of the autumn night:
I look in your eyes, you breathe my breath,
We rest together till dawn has come.

AUTUMNAL CLOUDS

Autumnal clouds,
Giant sheers of sunlight!
In the evening poise your vaporous pinnacles
Above the low horizon of October plains
And wait there until morning.
Then leap forward, O hollow-flanked hounds of the sky,
Upon your prey, and bite it in red joy!

Long have I searched for you, O clouds of change,
Tiger-striped clouds that in the sunset
Open your scarlet mouths and clash your teeth of flame!
Long have I expected you, O clouds, to spit your rain
Upon the trees bored with too long a blossoming,

[45]

Sending showers of sodden leaves reeling upon the grass,
To lie there like fallen kisses.

Autumnal clouds,
Giant gods of sunset!
See, beneath you, lakes like blue eyes where in mist
The somnolent trees cover hidden whispers of love;
See, beneath you, white swans diving and flashing
Like dreams of hands that meet and clasp and part from
    each other.
Come shake the woods and fill its trees with voices
Menacing and full of evil;
You shall not destroy this one immortal heart
Which I pour out to you, autumnal clouds,
To you and to the winter that shall be.

Soon shall I see you now, magnificent clouds,
Move rank on rank in armour of pearl and gold
Across the noisy earth shaken with tempest!
Soon shall your batteries break upon my heart,
Where it waits calm, wrapt in a dream of peace,
Amid the city hurling its towers at the sky.
Soon shall I hear your feet upon the roof-tops;
Soon shall I see your hands beat at the windows;
Soon shall your great arms clasp me; I shall die;
Die in a dream which cannot be of the earth.

Autumnal clouds,
Look! far there in the sunlight!
The glory floods you now, I see you plainly:

You are no more clouds to me, you are a woman,
White and rosy and gold and blue and beautiful.
You move across the sky, the dusk is at your feet,
The night is in your arms, the moon is on your breast,
The stars are in your eyes, the dawn is on your hair,
Drench me, drown me, darken me, make me drunken with
     deep red torrents of joy,
Till I forget all things in the world but this,
The glory of God everlasting, the fire of passion and death.

FAITH

The dark clouds gather around my path, they bar me in
     every way,
Every way but westward, where is the great sun's death;
But I do not fear those great dark clouds, nor the tragic
     death of a day,
My heart beats fully and steadily, faith is new-born with
     each breath;
Faith in that part of me which was not mine, which was
     given to me to use,
Which shall live on though all the suns fall dead into the
     night;
Faith in a love which rules all things: for though I fall and
     lose,
I shall live on for ever, for I have held with the light.

REUNION

Night after night I always come to you,
Darkness and distance do not ever divide us;
Nor the rainstorms nor bleak hills nor seas nor lightnings:
We lie together always until dawn,
Cheerfully, joyously, taking love from each other,
Naked as truth are our souls,
Our bodies are naked and pure.

I enter into your house without knocking,
With a smile you always greet me:
I know well you are all the world to me,
You know well I am all the world to you.
We know well we are together,
Love made us one—hate cannot ever change us.

We have not parted and we shall not part.

Night after night I always come to you,
For I have given to you my soul to cherish;
It is lost in you like a ship in the immense ocean.
You are the star to which my course is pointed,
You are the port to which my prow is lifted,
You are the beacon of my nights, the sun of my lone day-
    spring,
For my soul is safe with you unto eternity,
You will look after it—you will not let it stray aside.

Only to come and take of my soul from your lips,
That is all I need—and I come surely;

I shall be with you night on night for always:
You too will always see your soul in my own eyes.
You will run towards me on glad feet, smiling,
I know you are coming with the lamp, my darling;
Night after night I shall visit you for always:
And in this knowledge I can rest content.

ON THE BEACH

We lay together on the beach,
About us wavered and drifted the glittering stream of life:
The furious energy of childhood,
The mad assaults of lovers,
The tedious cares and worries of middle age,
The shock, and the final darkness.
And the sea rose and fell all about us,
Grey water upon grey water,
Darkly punctuating our utterance
With its bleak menace of death.

I am a ship departing;
Long farewells on the horizon:—
A tall dark ship
Feeling in its inmost fibres the wash of the sea.
And you are a weed on the beaches,
Or a strange beautiful sea-creature,
Pink and blue, dying
Because I am so far away.

The haze drifts about on the sea;
And the islands that rose in the morning,
Headland beyond white headland,
Are swallowed up in the afternoon.
Yet there seems floating near me
Something blue in the vast grey stillness;
And a lace handkerchief of white foam
Held close in a pale still hand.

With the blue glint of a diamond
The sun strikes upon the water;
Enkindling me, summoning me
To happiness and to despair;
To strange calm sorrows,
And to joys passing away with wet eyes.
Rings and dapples of foam
Seem washing over my heart,
And on my lips are the salt lips of the sea.

ON THE VERANDAH

Larkspur; windy July;
Trees riding up from the southward,
Green waves frozen before they fell,
Shattered with grey rifts of light:
Flickering in amber sunbeams,
Glinting with gold as the sunset passed;
We sat together and saw them change,
And in our hearts was peace.

In calm and opulent terraces
The sky unrolled ribbed cloud for us;
Marble-veined azure, peacefully walled.
Two and two went the grave white angels
Smiling and sometimes speaking to us:
The lower ones brooding in shadow,
The upper ones romping in sunlight,
Where like white ladders the light ran up
From the cellars to upper balconies,
Where with wind-blown daisies frail gardens bloomed in
    mid-air.

We watched them from the verandah,
Sitting together, you holding my hand;
The wind flapped the heavy bough-curtains,
And all our thoughts were at rest.
We were not troubled with anything,
We knew that this day was made for us,
We knew that new days would come in time,
The future and the past were now one.

Long we watched dark swallows hovering
Swift up the wind-waves of the sky,
Fluttering, soaring, and calling,
Wheeling like well-ordered oarsmen.
They passed through the sunpool washing the trees,
Rippling with warm heat over the world,
Caressing and changing the final faint clouds,
Before they receded to rest.

Evening bells sounded hollow, forlorn,
Out of a valley wreathed in white mist;
It was the time you must quit my side.
You went without pain or regret.
Such a perfect understanding ruled over our hearts
That, parting, I felt that you still held my hand;
For all of my life was known by you
In serene comprehensive surrender,
And I slept every night with no false dreams to mar my
  sleep.

IN THE GARDEN OF DREAMS

I wandered in the garden of my dreams:
Magnolias shook out waxen petals that burst
Against the glittering upthrust of strong green leaves.
There were glassy glaucous pools of green-blue water,
And columned poplars broken in the sky;
And in the midst a sarcophagus,
A rosy and golden sarcophagus,
A tomb of marble and bronze for us
To watch the swallows fly.

Heroes and warriors in armour
Guarded our solemn rest.
There we lay together safely,
Stone breast against stone breast;
Griffins with clutching paws
Lifted their beaks on high;

And in the midst a sarcophagus,
An impenetrable sarcophagus,
A tomb aloof, alone, for us
To watch the swallows fly.

I see sometimes sunlight flecking
The warm curves of your breast;
But you never turn to me with a smile,
And say, "Dear one, how do you rest?"
The magnolias drop cupped waxen petals
Against the breeze, with a sigh:
And in the midst is a sarcophagus,
A golden, cold sarcophagus,
A lofty forgotten tomb for us
To watch the swallows fly.

At night the stars like great white swans
Swim lazily overhead;
The guardians, weary of endless dawns,
Droop each a heavy head;
The bat flits amid the cypresses,
But we sleep deep on high;
And we are safe in our sarcophagus,
Our deep pale-grey sarcophagus,
Our tomb in the twilight made for us,
To watch, till the swallows fly.

THE OFFERING

It was when the autumn shook its heavy haze-curtains about
    us
(Dead leaves, dry leaves),
It was when the evenings were silent and their shadows came
    quick and easy,
That we walked in the garden together.
The autumn breeze lifted the fringes of its temple-brocades
    with a whisper;
And summoned us in to its secret.
No leaf fell from the mournful and shadow-clogged tree-
    tops,
No wild birds woke with a cry.

A cluster of sweet fresh violets
Gathered from cool spring valleys,
I lay on that autumn's grave.
Solitude and darkness
Have drawn over me deep curtains,
And in their folds I can sleep.

It was in the evening—pent evening of passion and sorrow—
(Dead leaves, dry leaves),
It was when the swollen rain-clouds waited upon the horizon,
That we parted from each other at last.
I found myself alone in that garden,
Dull mist hid the blurred tree-tops;
In the dim lake a heron slowly fluttered.
All my bitter secret forebodings
Rose and plucked me at the heart.

In dew-sprent sprays of heather
Wherein wild bees have murmured,
I gather you to my breast.
Beyond morose black headlands
I know grim seas are calling,
My time is up—I must go.

It was when the autumn drew its purple dream-curtains to-
    gether
(Dead leaves, dry leaves),
It was when the year turned seaward, like a great silent
    river proceeding,
That my memories returned to me.
Dark troops of memory,
Drear rain dashing against spent boughs.
It was in the autumn, in the evening,
That the clouds closed about my life.

A lonely violet aster
With heart of smouldering pollen
I press into your hand.
I have nothing more to offer but this,
This and the mad and secret
Love you have taken from me.

THE EMPTY DAYS

I

Along the street
In the afternoon,

Dismally perched on a crazy cart,
That creaks and wabbles dolefully,
With a starved white horse
Between the shafts,
Goes the giver of empty days.

The while he goes he blows his horn.
In the afternoon,
Golden and blue,
It bellows out
Over the world,
It swells unechoing,
Toneless and void.

But the people in the city scarcely stir to listen to it,
They know that he has nothing to offer them at all;
They know that long ago, on some black-visaged instant,
Their lives were crushed, their courage failed;
They have not even tears to weep at his slow passing,
The towers of aspiring reach wearily beyond to silence.
And between them and those towers there passes very slowly
Only the image of another empty day.

Along the street
In the afternoon,
Passes his shadow gaunt as death;
As he sits above
The shafts and rocks
His crazy head;
But it is not death he sells but days,

Long days, unchanged; grey, futile days.
But no one buys from him any more,
They would all rather have death instead.

To me he has given love that has failed and fallen
Into a soulless, cloudless depth of blue despair;
To me he too has offered
A Dead-Sea husk of memory that burns and dries my throat;
The ashes of opportunity burnt out, of experience shattered,
Drawn from the fires that once beat up and flared about me,
Until my foot no longer kicked a blue glow from their still-
        ness,
Not a single spark of warmth, nor a pang of misery.

Along the street
In the afternoon,
Blowing his futile horn that tears an ache from my heart—
His trump of doom—
Jogging behind a sickly horse,
And grinning at me,
Goes the giver of empty days.

II

Lonely sea that stretches out millions of curled tossing
        breakers,
To where my loved one waits;
Sea untravelled, sea that awaits in silence,
Open to me your gates;
Lend me your winds again that to the one I have not for-
        gotten

I may come and take a kiss;
Sea over which the light and shade fall evenly,
Grant me this.

Love has bound us together with scarlet threads of suffering,
Death only will make us twain.
Sea that has forgotten even the cause of its passion,
Tell me again
What white thing is that flitting out there in the distance,
What broken white thing that seeks?
Cold sea gleaming beneath your drifting shadows,
Why do you bare your teeth?

Lonely sea, forgotten, sailless in the morning,
Under unblinking sky;
Sea where the night has stalked weeping and raging with
    passion,
Into your dawn I fly;
Out over glittering, cold, inhuman distances,
To the gate where the east displays
Its immense beauty of violet-shrouded silence,
I go from my empty days.

III

The day when they brought the evil news to me,
Was one great turquoise over which the sun
Threw a strange network of golden threads that glinted
On the horizon, held in the cup of the sea;
And after the evil news was brought to me,

I went out to the beach where in the wet
The sun splashed coppery paints over the blue
Curled ruffles of the wave that beat beneath.

The horizon was hung in veils of violet haze;
They enclosed me from the one I sought apart.
I should have stayed with her—ah, the crape smoke
Of my regrets that blew across the seas!

But I would come again—a failing wave
After the full-tide mark was left upon the shore!
I had no love, nor hope, nor joy, nor heart;
I only knew, dully, that hope was dead;
I only knew, dully, that earth was fair;
I only knew, dully, my toil was lost.

IV

Quite patiently,
Content to wait,
Without complaint;
I sit and watch the empty days.

I am as one that is blinded
By marching too long against the sun;
Seeking too lofty cities
That are carven on its face.

Oh, sun of mine, enter my burnt-out heart;
Kindle the altar-fires

[59]

Death-flaming in the stillness
Of those black, polished walls.

Quite patiently,
Content to dream,
Without a word;
I sit and watch the day grow noon.

Out of the deep blue lake my memories rise;
They follow me beyond the rocky crest .
That swings up past the pines,
Where in an empty temple
Once long ago I stood with one
Whom I may never meet again.

Windflowers shatter in the quiet garden;
The asters break their stalks,
The roses crumple, fall.

Quite patiently,
Content with death;
Knowing I failed,
I pass through afternoon which is a dream.

Dim memories of the morning
Stir and rustle in my heart;—
Where is my day?

A bit of wreckage floated about the seas,
For days on days;

I moulder at last on some sand-pit, unnoted,
About me settle thoughts, my pale-grey gulls.

Quite patiently,
Content to wait;
I sit and watch the evening star
Slide, one white tear, into the night.

IN MEMORY OF A NIGHT

It was an hour before the dawn,
Barely a little hour before the dawn,
Long ago;
The moon was a full-sailed frigate in the ashen bay of the
    sky,
Swinging low,
The moon was slipping out with the cargo of my dreams.
I knew not if I waked or dreamed, nor cared to live or die.

Flicker and lurch of the train,
That tore me amain
Out of the steep dense-clustered trees
Into a valley walled with far light;
Breakers of night
Rising from buried seas.

It was an hour before the dawn,
Barely a little hour before the dawn,
That we lay clasping each other and dreamed awake at last;

[61]

Lip to eager lip and bodies pressing together,
One warm shuddering caress—but now all that is past:—
It is the dawn and I cannot rest,
The night is a dry fire gnawing through my breast.

A taxicab crashing
Down long deserted streets:
Files of light racing together to hurl themselves under the
    wheels;
The whole immense city tearing itself from me,
Because in the distance I see
Something that not even the city, nor seeking, nor my song
    reveals.

It is an hour before the dawn;
One fleeting beautiful hour before the dawn—
When the noise of the city and the false acclamations of
    men fall away from me;
I stand on a cool wind-washed summit,
Below me the whole green earth enkindles with ecstasy of
    light,
The sun throws a kiss over dark chasms packed with sullen
    sleep-mists rolling together,
And I hear the noise of far rain beating clamorous over the
    city,
And its sound is the falling of folded centuries slowly un-
    closing and dropping away.

In the midst of the city I builded,
Amid soft lights and smiles and rich flowers assembled,

My palace of dreams:—
There were feasts in my palace at evening and song **and**
full welcome of friends,
And new universes half hidden in the closing delights of **a**
kiss;
But now is an end of all this,
It is vanished like an old song that no one ends.

Flicker and toss of the train,
That tore me amain
Back to cold darkness from the warm light;
We who have laughed at the night,
Lip to eager lip and bodies pressing together,
Soft warm tremulous caresses of hand and of breast,
In the day's lurid pageant of gold and blue, we shall seek,
but shall not find, rest.

It was an hour before the dawn,
Barely a little hour before the dawn,
Long ago.
Long ago the sunlight kissed me—now I go as blind.
Would that I could find
If it was an empty dream, or was it as it seems?
The moon is rising high
Out of the last bay of the eastern sky,
With the cargo of my dreams.

EPILOGUE

Years have passed over me, whirling their whiplashes of
    days, since last I have written these lines.
Charioteers whooping, hallooing—their red wheels a flash in
    the dust;
The screaming and the neighing of horses biting each other
I did not heed, nor the dull echoes grinding and rumbling
Far down the pavements of eternity. All these were noth-
    ing to me,
But a shaking of torches out on the shores of the night;
Hissing sparks falling into the water—wet hands struggling,
    falling, and a low cry
Spreading out in great circles on stillness. Then the night
    closed down with its silence,
While the years went on screaming and curling their whips,
    on to their dark goal overhead.

There is no vision afloat in the boat of the night;
No ear ever hears
Distant waves breaking sullenly upon some low craggy shore,
Or tinkle of mandolins floating in harbors of dreams.
Outwards the clouds stream
Stretching out their dark necks and galloping, galloping for-
    ward,
While adrift
With the lamp long burnt out, and naught but the creak of
    the ropes
To mark each slow moment that gropes,

Ebbing out faintly, like afterglow's glimmer long held in
the arms of the west,
We drift or we rest;
Youth having passed away, age slowly passing, and whither
no soul of us knows:
But love never shows,
Through a rift in the west,
Dreams of some harbour whose red lamps repose
On the face of the waters, summoning our griefs to its breast.

But when the Sons of the Morning shall blow their great
golden trumpets, rending the red mist asunder,
And the trees with their flame-leaves of emerald and scarlet
shall leap out again at the sky,
All our dead passion and sorrow shall break into flame in
the grass,
And the flowering thereof shall be strewn 'neath the feet of
our God
Who shall walk out of the firmament, taking each life to
His breast;
And our souls like two flames irresistibly kindled, having
burnt through the last walls of space,
Shall shine in a circle of fire about His all-glorious Head
Who has ordered to sorrows an ending, and that Heaven
and Earth be made new.

PART THREE

CLIPPER SHIPS

Beautiful as a tiered cloud, skysails set and shrouds twanging, she emerges from the surges that keep running away before day on the low Pacific shore. With the roar of the wind blowing half a gale after, she heels and lunges, and buries her bows in the smother, lifting them swiftly, and scattering the glistening spray-drops from her jib-sails with laughter. Her spars are cracking, her royals are half splitting, her lower stunsail booms are bent aside, like bowstrings ready to loose, and the water is roaring into her scuppers, but she still staggers out under a full press of sail, her upper trucks enkindled by the sun into shafts of rosy flame.

Oh, the anchor is up and the sails they are set, and it's 'way Rio; 'round Cape Stiff and up to Boston, ninety days hauling at the ropes: the decks slope and the stays creak as she lurches into it, sending her jib awash at every thrust, and a handful of dust and a thirst to make you weep, are all we get for being two years away to sea.

Topgallant stunsail has carried away! Ease the spanker! The anchor is rusted on the deck. Men in short duck trousers, wide-brimmed straw hats, with brown mahogany faces, pace up and down, spinning the wornout yarns they told a year ago. Some are coiling rope; some smoke; "Chips"

[69]

is picking oakum near the boats. Ten thousand miles away lies their last port. In the rigging climbs a hairy monkey, and a green parakeet screams at the masthead. In the dead calm of a boiling noonday near the line, she lifts her spread of shining canvas from heel to truck, from jib o' jib to ringtail, from moonsails to watersails. Men have hung their washing in the stays so she can get more way on her. She ghosts along before an imperceptible breeze, the sails hanging limp in the cross-trees, and clashing against the masts. She is a proud white albatross skimming across the ocean, beautiful as a tiered cloud. Oh, a Yankee ship comes down the river; blow, boys, blow; her yards and masts they shine like silver; blow, my bully boys, blow; she's a crack ship, a dandy clipper, nine hundred miles from land; she's a down-Easter from Massachusetts, and she's bound to the Rio Grande!

Where are the men who put to sea in her on her first voyage? Some have piled their bones in California among the hides; some died frozen off the Horn in snowstorms; some slipped down between two greybacks, when the yards were joggled suddenly. Still she glistens beautifully, her decks snow-white with constant scrubbing as she sweeps into some empty sailless bay which sleeps all day, where the wild deer skip away when she fires her eighteen-pounder, the sound reverberating about the empty hills. San Francisco? No: San Francisco will not be built for a dozen years to come. Meanwhile she hums with the tumult of loading. The mutineers, even, are let out of their irons and flogged and fed. Every day from when the dawn flares up red amid the hills to the hour it drops dead to westward, men walk gawkily, balancing on their heads the burden of heavy, stiff hides. Now the anchor is up and the sails they are set, and it's 'way Rio. Boston girls are pulling at the ropes: only three months of trouble yet: time for us to go!

Beautiful as a tiered cloud she flies out seaward, and on her decks loaf and stumble a luckless crowd; the filthy sweepings of the stews. In a week, in a day, they have spent a year's wages, swilling it away and letting the waste of it run down among the gutters. How were these deadbeats bribed to go? Only the Ann Street runners know. Dagos, Dutchmen, Souwegians, niggers, crimp-captured greenhorns, they loaf up on the after-deck, some of them already wrecks, so sick they wish they had never been born. Before them all the "old man" calls for a bucket of salt water to wash off his shore face. While he is at it, telling them how he will haze them till they are dead if they try soldiering, but it will be good grub and easy work if they hand, reef, and steer, and heave the lead, his officers are below, rummaging through the men's dunnage, pulling out heavers, prickers, rum bottles, sheath knives, and pistols. On each grizzled half-cowed face appears something between a sheepish grin, a smirk of fear, a threat of treachery, and the dogged resignation of a brute. But the mate—Bucko Douglas is his name—is the very same that booted three men off the masthead when they were shortening sail in the teeth of a Cape Horn snorter.

[71]

Two of them fell into the sea, and the third was tossed still groaning into the water. Only last night the captain stuck his cigar butt into one poor swabber's face for not minding the compass, and gave Jim Baines a taste of ratline hash for coming up on deck with dirty hands. Meanwhile under a grand spread of canvas, one hundred feet from side to side, the ship rides up the parallels. From aloft through the blue stillness of a tropic night, crammed with stars, with thunder brewing in the horizon, a mournful echo rises and swells:

> Oh, my name is hanging Johnny,
> Hooray, hooray!
> Oh, my name is hanging Johnny,
> So hang, boys, hang.

The "Great Republic," launched before thirty thousand people, her main truck overlooking the highest steeple of the town, the eagle at her bows, and colours flying, now in her first and last port, is slowly dying. She is a charred hulk, with toppling masts, seared gliding, and blistered sides. The "Alert" no more slides pertly through the bergs of the Horn. The desolate barrens of Staten Land, where no man was ever born, hold her bones. The Black Baller "Lightning," that took eighty thousand dollars' worth of cargo around the world in one quick trip, was hurled and ripped to pieces on some uncharted reef or other. The "Dreadnought" disappeared in a hurricane's smother of foam. The "Sovereign of the Seas," that never furled her topsails for ten years, was sheared clean amidships by the bows of an iron steamer as she left her last port. The slaver, "Bald Eagle," cut an unlucky career short when she parted with her anchor and piled up on the Paracels where the pirate junks are waiting for every ship that swells out over the horizon. The "Antelope" was caught off the Grand Ladrone in the northeast monsoon; she's gone. The "Flying Cloud," proud as she was of beating every ship that carried the Stars and Stripes or the St. George's flag, could not race faster than a thunderbolt that fell one day on her deck and turned her to a cloud of flame—everything burned away but her fame! No more will California hear the little "Pilgrim's" parting cheer. The crew took to an open boat when their ship was scuttled by a privateer. So they die out, year after year.

Sometimes the lookout on a great steamer wallowing and threshing through the heavy seas by night, sees far off on his lee quarter something like a lofty swinging light. Beautiful as a tiered cloud, a ghostly clipper-ship emerges from the surges that keep running away before day on the low Pacific shore. Her upper works are enkindled by the sun into shafts of rosy flame. Swimming like a duck, steering like a fish, easy yet dry, lively yet stiff, she lifts cloud on cloud of crowded stainless sail. She creeps abeam, within hail, she dips, she chases, she outpaces like a mettlesome racer the lumbering tea-kettle that keeps her company. Before she fades into the weather quarter, the lookout cries: "Holy Jiggers, are you the Flying Dutchman, that you go two knots to our one?" Hoarsely comes back this answer from the sail: "Challenge is our name: America our nation: Bully Waterman our master: we can beat Creation."

    And it's 'way Rio;
    Way—hay—hay, Rio;
    O, fare you well, my pretty young girl,
    For we're bound to the Rio Grande.

DOWN THE MISSISSIPPI

I. EMBARKATION

Dull masses of dense green,
The forests range their sombre platforms;
Between them silently, like a spirit,
The river finds its own mysterious path.

Loosely the river sways out, backward, forward,
Always fretting the outer side;
Shunning the invisible focus of each crescent,
Seeking to spread into shining loops over fields.

Like an enormous serpent, dilating, uncoiling,
Displaying a broad scaly back of earth-smeared gold;
Swaying out sinuously between the dull motionless forests,
As molten metal might glide down the lip of a vase of dark
    bronze;

It goes, while the steamboat drifting out upon it,
Seems now to be floating not only outwards but upwards;
In the flight of a petal detached and gradually moving sky-
    ward
Above the pink explosion of the calyx of the dawn.

II. HEAT

As if the sun had trodden down the sky,
Until it holds living air no more, but only humid vapor,
Heat pressing upon earth with irresistible languor,
Turns all the solid forest into half-liquid smudge.

The heavy clouds like cargo-boats strain slowly against its
    current;
And the flickering of the heat-haze is like the thunder of ten
    thousand paddles
Against the heavy wall of the horizon, pale blue and utterly
    windless,
Whereon the sun hangs motionless, a brassy disk of flame.

III. FULL MOON

Flinging its arc of silver bubbles, quickly shifts the moon
From side to side of us as we go down its path;
I sit on the deck at midnight and watch it slipping and
    sliding,
Under my tilted chair, like a thin film of spilt water.

It is weaving a river of light to take the place of this river;
A river where we shall drift all night, then come to rest
in its shallows;
And then I shall wake from my drowsiness and look down
from some dim treetop
Over white lakes of cotton, like moonfields on every side.

IV. THE MOON'S ORCHESTRA

When the moon lights up
Its dull red campfire through the trees;
And floats out, like a white balloon,
Into the blue cup of the night, borne by a casual breeze;
The moon-orchestra then begins to stir.
Jiggle of fiddles commence their crazy dance in the dark-
ness:
Crickets churr
Against the stark reiteration of the rusty flutes which frogs
Puff at from rotted logs
In the swamp.
And then the moon begins her dance of frozen pomp
Over the lightly quivering floor of the flat and mournful
river.
Her white feet slightly twist and swirl.
She is a mad girl
In an old unlit ballroom
Whose walls, half-guessed at through the gloom,
Are hung with the rusty crape of stark black cypresses
Which show, through gaps and tatters, red stains half hid-
den away.

[76]

V. THE STEVEDORES

Frieze of warm bronze that glides with catlike movement
Over the gangplank poised and yet awaiting,
The sinewy thudding rhythm of forty shuffling feet
Falling like muffled drumbeats on the stillness.
O roll the cotton down,
Roll, roll the cotton down,
From the further side of Jordan,
O roll the cotton down!

And the river waits,
The river listens,
Chuckling its little banjo-notes that break with a flop on the
    stillness;
And by the low dark shed that holds the heavy freights,
Two lonely cypresses stand up and point with stiffened fingers
Far southward where a single chimney stands out aloof in
    the sky.

VI. NIGHT LANDING

After the whistle's roar has bellowed and shuddered,
Shaking the sleeping town and the somnolent river,
The deep-toned floating of the pilot's bell
Suddenly warns the engines.

They stop like heart-beats that abruptly stop,
The shore glides to us in a wide low curve.

And then—supreme revelation of the river—
The tackle is loosed—the long gangplank swings outwards—

[77]

And poised at the end of it, half-naked beneath the search-
light,
A blue-black negro with gleaming teeth waits for his chance
to leap.

VII. THE SILENCE

There is a silence I carry about with me always;
A silence perpetual, for it is self-created;
A silence of heat, of water, of unchecked fruitfulness
Through which each year the heavy harvests bloom, and
burst and fall.

Deep, matted green silence of my South,
Often within the push and scorn of great cities,
I have seen that mile-wide waste of water swaying out to
you,
And on its current glimmering, I am going to the sea.

There is a silence I have achieved: I have walked beyond
its threshold;
I know it is without horizons, boundless, fathomless, perfect.
And some day maybe, far away,
I will curl up in it at last and sleep an endless sleep.

THE OLD SOUTH

High streaks of cottony-white cloud fill the sky. The sun
slips out of the swamp swinging his heavy-jewelled
mace before his face as he plays with the ripples that

gurgle under the rotting cypress-knees. The breeze lifts the Spanish moss an instant and then is still. The sun tosses dew over the ragged palmetto-leaves. Aslant on a gush of warm breeze from the broiling savannah, the song of a mockingbird floats, a fierce scurry of notes, through the air. The sun seems to be kindling a flare at every point of the horizon. Grasshoppers, crickets, cicadas, everything that flits or skims, tunes and trills its shrill violin. Butterflies flutter, broken motes of color; hummingbird and dragon-fly dart green streaks through the quivering sky.

The river rolls, boiling and frothing through the lowlands. It is weary of the dull stiff mudbanks that flake away before it in sticky chips; weary of the turbid masses of mud that it must scour away to make its path down to the sea. It gulps and seethes horribly with hungry angry lips, fretting first one bank, then another, as it goes sliding and flopping down the long twisted bends in the fierce glare of morning, deceived no longer at each marsh-outlet and creek and bayou-mouth into thinking that here and not further south must be the clear blue water it seeks, where its heavy burden may fall in peace. The river goes slapping, lapping, rustling the canes of the brake and the motionless cypress-trees. A mockingbird's song floats down before it in the breeze.

It is noon and the carnival, king of fools, rules the city. A beautiful woman, her face cold, haughty, expressionless, the fire in her eyes half hidden, goes dancing down the street with a man whose shape is like an ape. Her feet stir the dust and it glitters as it settles in streams over her shoulders, like slipping confetti-showers. She is a flower over-weary of the sun. Her perfume is almost gone, and the fever will soon snap her from her stalk and toss her into the tomb. Bass drums toll to her tripping movement. Her skirts sway. Amid their flickering spangles plays a satyr, grinning at the multitude. He tears off her frills and flings them into the gutter choked with filth. Her half-naked form writhes and recoils like a tree before the storm.

The river frowns and lours for a heavy, fuming, dull blue shower races gloomily above it from the northward. As it goes it throws out at the trees tentacles of curled coppery lightning that enlace and line the branches and send them crashing downwards with full powdery explosions of muffled thunder. The river lashes itself into fits, smashing the bank with maddened fists, as it spins the quivering steamer around and nearly sends it reeling aground. It growls, it howls, it shouts its terror of the forest whose broken logs topple into it with a great splash, swirling and whirling, sucked and crashing in sudden black somersaults, while the storm roars and grumbles away with spattered hail bullets and noise of affray. Now the forest groans and drips and shrieks with rain that whistles through its branches. Every trickle, every pool, every creek is full. The choked-up torrent overflows and covers miles on miles of furrows and woods with endless glaring wastes of water. A gaunt pine falls with a sigh and a splash.

Slowly the river resumes its patient march through the lowlands. Now autumn comes, and afternoon seems throwing grey filaments of haze from tree to tree. The old plantation sleeps, for it has nothing else to do. Live oaks are bowered about it, drooping heavily, weary of holding up lusty green leaves from year to year. In graves under the live oaks many are sleeping. They have slipped from the dream of life to the dream of death. Perhaps they died for a woman's sake, for a sigh, a chance word, a look, a letter, for nothing, or for a song that men sing.\ What matter? Life is a dream; to-day, to-morrow, yesterday, it is the same. Along old floors underneath mouldering doors blow light gusts of wind stirring the dust. A mouse cheeps in a corner. Old age creeps upon us, and life is grey. The old plantation moulders, day on day. Soon there will be gaps in the floors and the doors will swing open to all. Let us doze on the levee and feel the breeze as it slips down the river running past us.

The river runs very fast, for it is bearing sodden logs, like broken lives. The sleepy buzzards line the grey cottonwoods that tower above its banks. To them, too, life is a dream. This morning they tore the rank carrion of a dead horse that floated down to them. Death does not matter, for life is defeat, but it is very sweet to have plenty to eat and to sleep in the sunlight. Sleeping and waking and sleeping again, that is how one learns to live without pain. Let autumn throw thin filaments of regret from tree to tree. Leaves may drop slowly, but the live oak which drops not its leaves at all is the tree that is planted on graves.

Immortal death is very sweet
When brown leaves fill the dripping gap
Of a broken vault, and the frightened feet
Of mice pit-patter, and owls flap
Out to the cool moonshiny night,
Which scatters crushed jewels down the river;
While trees, dumb-stricken ghosts in flight,
Chatter and shake against each other.

Tinkle—tinkle—drop; the rain that filters through the leaky
roof. Under the colonnade where slaves were sold and
bars chinked with gold runs a tiny stream of water
through the dust. Was that a door slamming or only
a torn hanging that flapped? Who knows? Perhaps it
was two ghosts who chattered together through agued
lips and rattling teeth? Not a dusty bottle in the bar.
Marks of muddy boots on the smashed marble. Wind
that laughs insanely up the spiral stairways, down the
floorless corridors. Let us go, for rain is dropping and
the roof is leaking, and I seem to hear a grey frog hop-
ping while yonder door is creaking as if someone were
locked behind it and were whispering to get out. Let
us go, for the ceiling sags and will soon be falling, and
a black spider is crawling past my face, and rags are
drifting about on the floor. Let us go, for a crazy deaf
woman with a bent stick threatens us in quavering
voice, declaring she will strike us for daring to enter
her palace. Let us go and not come back any more.
The dead are best dead and forgotten.
The river rolls through fields blossoming with cotton day

after day. In a crazy cabin someone is crooning a song. The sun lifts his long jewelled mace an instant, in careless lazy fingers, before his face and lets it slip away again. Aslant on a chill scurry of rain floats a mockingbird's jangled song. It dies away and leaves only silence, half-enclosing the monotonous drone of a sad hymn of despair which a sleepy negro is humming to himself from nowhere.

THE PASSING OF THE SOUTH

On a catafalque, draped in black, under bronze cannon, forlorn and white, rigid in death, the corpse of the South is borne to its tomb. With muffled drums, with arms reversed, the veterans gather gaunt and grey, and their close-furled flags, 'neath the sun's pale flash, droop in weary folds to-day.

Eighteen hundred and sixty-one, and the sun shines gaily. The new levies of the North are swarming out from Washington, southwestward, to Bull Run. Listen to the drum as it rumble-bumbles through the woods, windless but cool, in the heat of July. Look at the clean blue uniforms, the epaulets, the brass buttons, the sashes with their thick gold braid. Let's go and picnic in the woods—who's afraid? "Our boys will shoot and the rebels will scoot, and day after to-morrow John Brown's body will be marching into Richmond. Then we'll hang Jeff Davis from a sour apple tree, as we go marching on." The sun flashes, but the leaves are silent. Suddenly

the yell of a panther cuts the air, and from everywhere
bursts out at once grey smoke and the drumming roll
of a volley. Little grey figures are stealing out of the
woods. They rise and shoot, disappear into the undergrowth, rise and shoot again, near and more near. And
still rises more menacing that long scream of a cheer
and a red banner, with long blue bars, studded with
stars, bursts out of the woods and flickers through the
smoke upon the left. "Fire—fire—for God's sake fire—
what are you holding that gun for! Where—there—
everywhere—the yell is on both sides of us—fire up in
the air! Back—back—they are on our flank—make
tracks for Washington—Father Abe is there—he will
save us! Hoofbeats—cavalry—the cavalry are in pur-
suit—every man for himself—why don't they fall down
when we shoot—may God curse that sun that glared
in our faces—may the devil take this gun, it's too heavy
to carry. Back—back—has anyone thought of the flag
—no, it's gone with the rest. Back—back to Washington!"

On a catafalque, draped in black, under bronze cannon, forlorn and white, rigid in death, the corpse of the South
is borne to its tomb. With a low roll of drums and the
dull tramp of feet, the procession starts, and it dribbles
slowly down the long street, followed by sobs from
broken hearts.

Eighteen hundred and sixty-two, and the new President of
the Confederate States is present at a grand review of
his army. From a fair knoll overlooking the scene, he
sees afar the green fields, covered with long grey files

of troops, a band of brothers assembled to defend the ascendant star of the South. Here are the cavalry of Virginia, men on blooded horses, which their orderlies have curried and groomed till they shine like silver. These are the men ready to ride for a jest into the cannon's mouth. Their sabres click, and their horses curvet and prance and seem to curtsey as they dance in the sunlight. Here is the light artillery of Louisiana —the swamp-tigers, dark men, sitting erect on the caissons, rumbling at a gallop over the field. Here are the tall hunters, from Tennessee and Arkansas, sallow, rangy men able to draw a bead on a squirrel's eye at thirty paces. Here comes, thundering and straining at the traces, the heavy artillery of South Carolina, the men who battered Fort Sumter to pieces. They are singing of Charleston girls and the dust rises and curls about their wheels. The whole earth quivers and reels, and the President bows and smiles. The grey files of hoarsely singing men, swinging at a rapid pace out of the dust, seem like endless phantoms, turning and returning again. The President rides forward and the movement of the troops is stopped. "You are the seed-corn of the Confederacy," he says, "which we will soon plant in the North." A roar breaks forth and is blent with the baggage-wagons at the ends of the horizon. The whole army gives its assent.

On a catafalque, draped in black, under bronze cannon, forlorn and white, rigid in death, the corpse of the South is borne to its tomb. Boom!—they have reached the cemetery and the artillery is firing the last salute while the coffin in its single great flag is slowly lowered to the grave. The drooping banners, with their staffs shrouded in crape, are like great top-heavy flowers falling into the black hole in the ground. Boom!—old men used to battle hear that sound and they clutch with long bony hands their crutches, while the tears start. Boom! It is almost dark.

Eighteen hundred and sixty-three and Lee has a new plan. Grant is holding Vicksburg in a ring of fire and steel and the South is beginning to feel the pinch. The Mississippi is almost gone. Unless England comes soon to our help, we cannot fight on. Forward then, the South! In one last desperate effort, sweep up through Pennsylvania and outflank the Capitol! Every night, men going to bed see afar the campfires of innumerable invading armies, like fireflies in the hills. Philadelphia fills with panic and the tramp of hastily drilling men. But on Seminary Ridge, before Gettysburg, Lee comes to a halt. There from Little Round Top to the Bloody Angle, stand the armies of Meade. Speak, guns! One hundred and twenty-five cannon fill the valley for three hours with swirling drifts of death. Now, then, Pickett, Longstreet, Heth! Forward—charge! Forward—charge! With bands playing and colours flying, dyeing the grass with their blood. "O I'll live and die for Dixie— Hooray—Hooray—I'll live and die"—the wind bears the clamor away.

Dust that rises—dust that settles—and the rust of ancient years . . .

On a catafalque, draped in black, under bronze cannon, forlorn and white, rigid in death, the corpse of the South
is borne to its tomb.

IN THE CITY OF NIGHT

(TO THE MEMORY OF EDGAR ALLAN POE)

City of night,
Wrap me in your folds of shadow.

City of twilight,
City that projects itself into the west,
City whose columns rest upon the sunset, city of square,
threatening masses blocking out the light:
City of twilight,
Wrap me in your folds of shadow.

City of midnight, city that the full moon overflows,
City where the cats prowl and the closed iron dust-carts go
rattling through the shadows:
City of midnight,
Wrap me in your folds of shadow.

City of early morning, cool fresh-sprinkled city, city whose
sharp roof peaks are splintered against the stars, city
that unbars tall haggard gates in pity,
City of midnight,
Wrap me in your folds of shadow.

City of rain, city where the bleak wind batters the hard drops once and again, sousing a shivering, cursing beggar who clings amid the stiff Apostles on the cathedral portico;

City where the glare is dull and lowering, city where the clouds flare and flicker as they pass onwards, where sputtering lamps stare into the muddy pools beneath them;

City where the winds shriek up the streets and tear into the squares, city whose cobbles quiver and whose pinnacles waver before the buzzing chatter of raindrops in their flight;

City of midnight,
Drench me with your rain of sorrow.

City of vermilion curtains, city whose windows drip with crimson, tawdry, tinselled, sensual city, throw me pitilessly into your crowds.

City filled with women's faces leering at the passers-by,

City with doorways always open, city of silks and swishing laces, city where bands bray dance-music all night in the plaza,

City where the overscented light hangs tepidly, stabbed with jabber of the crowd, city where the stars stare coldly, falsely smiling through the smoke-filled air,

City of midnight,
Smite me with your despair.

City of emptiness, city of the white façades, city where one
   lonely dangling lantern wavers aloft like a taper before
   a marble sarcophagus, frightening away the ghosts;
City where a single white-lit window in a motionless blackened housefront swallows the hosts of darkness that
   stream down the street towards it;
City above whose dark tree-tangled park emerges suddenly,
   unlit, uncannily, a grey ghostly tower whose base is
   lost in the fog, and whose summit has no end,

City of midnight,
Bury me in your silence.

City of night,
Wrap me in your folds of shadow.

City of restlessness, city where I have tramped and wandered,
City where the herded crowds glance at me suspiciously, city
   where the churches are locked, the shops unopened, the
   houses without hospitality,

City of restlessness,
Wrap me in your folds of shadow.

City of sleeplessness, city of cheap airless rooms, where in the
   gloom are heard snorers through the partition, lovers
   who struggle, couples that squabble, cabs that rattle,
   cats that squall,

City of sleeplessness,
Wrap me in your folds of shadow.

City of feverish dreams, city that is being besieged by all the
    demons of darkness, city of innumerable shadowy vaults
    and towers, city where passion flowers desperately, and
    treachery ends in death the story,

City of night,
Wrap me in your folds of shadow.

ARIZONA POEMS

I. THE WELL IN THE DESERT

By the well in the desert I sat for long,
And watched the magpies, with black-and-white checkered
    bodies,
Leaping from twig to twig of the greasewood
To look at the water spilled on the ground
By the herder who went by with three lean cattle,
Climbing out of the blue-and-gold silence of morning.
There was the low well with stones piled about it,
The coarse tattered rope, the battered tin bucket,
And the nose of my pony cropping thin grass not far off;
Then grey sagebrush and silence.
At the horizon
The heat rose and fell,
Sharp flickering arpeggios;
The wind started up somewhere,

[90]

Then stopped.
The blue smoke of my cigarette
Wavered and failed.
I was drowsing.
And it seemed to me in my dream
That I was riding
To a low brown cluster of squat adobe houses
Under the eaves of a red barren mesa,
Where the track of a wagon trail paused, dipped, and van-
    ished
By a corral of rough plastered stone:
And I saw in my dream,
Looking down at the houses,
An Indian with a red sash, flannel shirt and blue trousers,
And a red band about his coarse black hair.
Eyes dark as an antelope's
Looked up at me:
Sheep were feeding about him.
And I said to him, "Where do you come from?"
And he replied,
"From Nazareth, beyond the desert,
In Galilee."

II. MEXICAN QUARTER

By an alley lined with tumble-down shacks,
And street-lamps askew, half-sputtering,
Feebly glimmering on gutters choked with filth and dogs
Scratching their mangy backs:
Half-naked children are running about,
Women puff cigarettes in black doorways,

Crickets are crying.
Men slouch sullenly
Into the shadows:
Behind a hedge of cactus,
The smell of a dead horse
Mingles with the smell of bacon-fat frying.

And a girl in a black lace shawl
Sits in a rickety chair by the square of an unglazed window,
And sees the explosion of the stars
Softly poised on the velvet sky.
And she is humming to herself:—
"Stars, if I could reach you
(You are so very clear that it seems as if I could reach you),
I would give you all to the Madonna's image,
On the grey-plastered altar behind the paper flowers,
So that Juan would come back to me,
And we could live again those lazy burning hours,
Forgetting the tap of my fan and my sharp words.
And I would only keep four of you,
Those two blue-white ones overhead,
To hang in my ears;
And those two orange ones yonder,
To fasten on my shoe buckles."

A little further along the street
A man sits stringing a brown guitar.
The smoke of his cigarette curls 'round his head,
And he too is humming, but other words:
"Think not that at your window I wait;

New love is better, the old is turned to hate.
Fate! Fate! All things pass away;
Life is forever, youth is for a day.
Love again if you may
Before the stars are blown out of the sky,
And the crickets die!
Babylon and Samarkand
Are mud walls in a waste of sand."

III. CLIFF-DWELLING

The canyon is choked with stones and undergrowth;
The heat that falls from the sky
Beats at the walls, slides, and reverberates
Down in a wave of grey dust and white fire,
Stinging the mouth and eyes.

The ponies struggle and scramble,
Halfway up, along the canyon wall;
Their listless riders seldom lift
A weary hand to guide their feet;
Stones are loosened and clatter
Down to the sunbaked depths.

Nothing has ever lived here,
Nothing could ever live here;
Two hawks, screaming and wheeling,
Rouse the eyes to look aloft.

Boldly poised in a shelf of the stone,
Tiny walls peer down on us:
Towers with little square windows.

When we plod up to them,
And dismounting, fasten our horses,
Suddenly a blue-grey flock of doves
Burst in a flutter of wings from the shadows.

Shards of pots and shreds of straw,
Empty brush-roofed rooms in darkness;
And the sound of water tinkling,
A clock that ticks the centuries off to silence.

IV. THE WINDMILLS

The windmills, like great sunflowers of steel,
Lift themselves proudly over the straggling houses;
And at their feet the deep blue-green alfalfa
Cuts the desert like the stroke of a sword.

Yellow melon flowers
Crawl beneath the withered peach-trees;
A date-palm throws its heavy fronds of steel
Against the scoured metallic sky.

The houses, double-roofed for coolness,
Cower amid the manzanita scrub.
A man with jingling spurs
Walks heavily out of a vine-bowered doorway,
Mounts his pony, rides away.

[94]

The windmills stare at the sun.
The yellow earth cracks and blisters.
Everything is still.

In the afternoon
The wind takes dry waves of heat and tosses them,
Mingled with dust, up and down the streets,
Against the belfry with its green bells:

And, after sunset, when the sky
Becomes a green and orange fan,
The windmills, like great sunflowers on dried stalks,
Stare hard at the sun they cannot follow.

Turning, turning, forever turning
In the chill night-wind that sweeps over the valley,
With the shriek and the clank of the pumps groaning be-
    neath them,
And the choking gurgle of tepid water.

THE GRAND CANYON OF THE COLORADO

I

I have seen that which is mysterious,
Aloof, divided, silent;
Something not of this earth.

Suddenly the endless dark green piny uplands
Stopped.

Yellow, red, grey-green, purple-black chasms fell swiftly
    below each other.

On the other side,
Strong-built, arose
Towers whose durable terraces were hammered from red
    sandstone,
Purple granite, and gold.

Beyond
A golden wall.
Aloof, inscrutable.

It was hidden
Behind layers of white silence.
No voice might reach it;
It was not of this earth.

II

When the free thunder-spirit
Had built and carved these terraced walls,
Completing his task of ages;
He wrote upon them
In dark invisible words:
"It is finished."

Silent and windless,
The forever completed
Is never broken but by clouds.
Sometimes dark eagles, slow-sailing,

[96]

Rise out of it, like spirits,
Wheeling away.

Now in the steady glare,
Some will moves darkly,
Driving the clouds, piling them,
Shaping masses of shadow
That move slowly forward
Over the array of towers.

Yet still behind them,
Unscarred, unaltered,
The work stands finished;
Without a cry of protest, for protest is uncompletion,
Moulded and fashioned forever in durable ageless stone.
And on every surface is written
In strong invisible words:
"It is finished."

III

Should I by chance deserve some last reward from earth,—
The rewards of earth are usually unwholesome,—
One single thing I would ask for,
Burn my body here.

Kindle the pyre
Upon this jutting point
Dry aromatic juniper,
Lean flame, blue smoke,
Ashes and dust.

The winds would drift the ash
Outwards across the canyon;
To the rose-purple rim of the desert
Beyond the red-barred towers.

The rabbits in the morning
Would come and snuff at the embers,
While the chasm, rekindling,
Would build up its silent poem of color to the sun.

IV

Shadows of clouds
March across the canyon,
Shadows of blue hands passing
Over a curtain of flame.

Clutching, staggering, upstriking,
Darting in blue-black fury,
To where the pinnacles, green and orange,
Await.

The winds are battling and striving to break them;
Thin lightnings spit and flicker.
The peaks seem a dance of scarlet demons
Flitting amid the shadows.

Grey rain-curtains wave afar off,
Wisps of vapour curl and vanish;
The sun throws soft shafts of golden light
Over rose-buttressed palisades.

Now the clouds are a lazy procession:
Blue balloons bobbing solemnly
Over black-draped walls:

Where rise sharp-fretted, golden-roofed cathedrals
Exultantly, and split the sky with light.

LINCOLN

I

Like a gaunt, scraggly pine
Which lifts its head above the mournful sandhills;
And patiently, through dull years of bitter silence,
Untended and uncared for, starts to grow.

Ungainly, laboring, huge,
The wind of the north has twisted and gnarled its branches;
Yet in the heat of mid-summer days, when thunder clouds
    ring the horizon,
A nation of men shall rest beneath its shade.

And it shall protect them all,
Hold everyone safe there, watching aloof in silence;
Until at last, one mad stray bolt from the zenith
Shall strike it in an instant down to earth.

There was a darkness in this man, an immense and hollow
    darkness,
Of which we may not speak, nor share with him nor enter;
A darkness through which strong roots stretched downwards
    into the earth
Towards old things;

Towards the herdsman-kings who walked the earth and
    spoke with God,
Towards the wanderers who sought for they knew not what,
    and found their goal at last;
Towards the men who waited, only waited patiently when
    all seemed lost,
Many bitter winters of defeat;

Down to the granite of patience,
These roots swept, knotted fibrous roots, prying, piercing,
    seeking,
And drew from the living rock and the living waters about
    it,
The red sap to carry upwards to the sun.

Not proud, but humble,
Only to serve and pass on, to endure to the end through
    service,
For the axe is laid at the roots of the trees, and all that bring
    not forth good fruit
Shall be cut down on the day to come and cast into the fire.

III

There is a silence abroad in the land to-day,
And in the hearts of men, a deep and anxious silence;
And, because we are still at last, those bronze lips slowly
    open,
Those hollow and weary eyes take on a gleam of light.

Slowly a patient, firm-syllabled voice cuts through the end-
    less silence,
Like laboring oxen that drag a plough through the chaos
    of rude clay-fields;
"I went forward as the light goes forward in early spring,
But there were also many things which I left behind.

"Tombs that were quiet;
One, of a mother, whose brief light went out in the darkness,
One of a loved one, the snow on whose grave is long falling,
One only of a child, but it was mine.

"Have you forgotten your graves? Go, question them in
    anguish,
Listen long to their unstirred lips. From your hostages to
    silence
Learn there is no life without death, no dawn without sun-
    setting,
No victory but to him who has given all."

The clamor of cannon dies down, the furnace-mouth of the
    battle is silent,
The midwinter sun dips and descends, the earth takes on
    afresh its bright colors.
But he whom we mocked and obeyed not, he whom we
    scorned and mistrusted,
He has descended, like a god, to his rest.

Over the uproar of cities,
Over the million intricate threads of life wavering and cross-
    ing,
In the midst of problems we know not, tangling, perplexing,
    ensnaring,
Rises one white tomb alone.

Beam over it, stars,
Wrap it 'round, stripes—stripes red for the pain that he bore
    for you—
Enfold it forever, O flag, rent, soiled, but repaired through
    your anguish;
Long as you keep him there safe, the nations shall bow to
    your law.

Strew over him flowers:
Blue forget-me-nots from the north and the bright pink
    arbutus
From the east, and from the west rich orange blossom,
But from the heart of the land take the passion-flower;

Rayed, violet, dim,
With the nails that pierced, the cross that he bore and the
    circlet,
And beside it there lay also one lonely snow-white magnolia,
Bitter for remembrance of the healing which has passed.

PART FOUR

THE LAST FRONTIER

Having passed over the world,
And seen three seas and two mountains,
He came to the last frontier.

On a hilltop
There were two men making a hole in the ground:
And beside it, his own dead body lay.

The thin man stroked his beard,
And wondered if the grave was deep enough;
The fat man sweated and dug,
And longed for a glass of beer.

Meantime his body lay there,
In a shabby suit, on a bed of wet leaves.
And the clouds of the evening, blown from beyond the
    world,
Swung lightly past his face.

But he waited until
The body was dropped and the earth shovelled deep upon
    it:
The lean man put up a cross,
The fat man stumped off home.

Then he went back from the last frontier
To the countries he had known years ago;
To the palaces of night and the peaks ringed with fire,
Without hope.

THE SWAN

Under a wall of bronze,
Where beeches dip and trail
Thin branches in the water,
With red-tipped head and wings,
A beaked ship under sail,
There glides a great black swan.

Under the autumn trees
He goes. The branches quiver,
Dance in the wraith-like water,
Which ripples beneath the sedge
With the slackening furrow that glides
In his wake when he is gone:
The beeches bow dark heads.

Into the windless dusk,
Where in mist great towers stand
Guarding a lonely strand
That is bodiless and dim,
He speeds with easy stride;
And I would go beside,
Till the low brown hills divide
At last, for me and him.

THE CATARACT

There was a man who said he saw a cataract in the mountains,
Its sides were jade and silver and its waters molten gold.
Afar it shone, that living wall of water,
Laughing, leaping downwards to the blue gulf below.
And in its tones there was the clang of metal,
Bells shattered on sheer granite, bells burst in falling spray;
Bells in the sweeping fern, the golden rush of water
Into a pine-filled valley, up whose splintered slopes he
    crawled.
Upwards or down he could not go, an ice-slope barred for
    ever
All hope of further movement; no bird could pass that way;
He watched that cataract freezing, crawled back, and long
    years later
He made a song about it, ten centuries ago.

GULF STREAM

I was born on the banks of the green Gulf Stream,
Where the Mississippi discharges its turbid waters
Into the sea, fringed 'round with palm-clad islands,
The home of the hurricane, where the shark darts from afar;
I was born with the song of the wind in my ears,
In the flash of the staggering combers, where the surf breaks
    on the shore,
I opened my eyes and saw the palm-fronds swaying,

The live oak rustle its dark green leaves, the log-wood
    blossom burn red.

Weed that tangles and weed that drifts,
Shreds of brown in the blue-green water,
Shrivelled, lank on a blazing beach,—
Laughter!—
Wind that pipes in the royal shrouds;
Dead men's bones on a spit of sand,
Parakeets that flash and scream
Past the warring palms, forever.

I will arise in the night and look on the stars;
Orion and the Pleiades southward ascending,
South-east, north-west, the path of the Milky Way:—
Sargasso-weed blown over the void of heaven.
The wind is tossing thin racks of cloud like masses of foam;
Between them, topaz and emerald and icy white,
The constellations blaze and are blotted out;
Like sparks that float in the sea on a tropic night.

Stars that swim by night in the dim Gulf Stream;
Wave that uprises, vast wall and valley of water;
Peak-surrounded blue islands
Crumbling away in the void;
Chasm of silence out of which the wind surges,
Night on the deck and the moist salty gust in my hair;
Ship of my soul that steadily sails down the current,
To lonely north oceans, making old landfalls more fair.

I have heard coastlands speak to the oncoming ocean;
I have heard granite shiver like harp-strings heavily stricken,
Ground-bass of the wind that breaks
In desperate fury
On islands of fire whereon the sun burns madly,
Down valleys of pineapple fringed with orange blossom;
Lagoons, blue lakes of quivering light half-hidden
Under the silence of the nodding palms.

A ship alone at daybreak
Lost in the splendour of a tossing ocean;
Blue glassy floors that slide
Like silk beneath its keel;
A ship that restless drives
With sky-sails towards morning;
Where the sun rising pales the vast horizon,
As from his forehead fanwise streams the glory of the light.

SUNSET

The sea uprose,
Wave after wave, nine waves behind each other;
The sky shut down,
A giant's spread-out hand;
And, in between,
There was another country:
Miles on miles of islands stretched out naked ridges
In the windless desolation
Of a shadowless red ocean
Where no sail had ever been.

[111]

SALEM COLLEGE LIBRARY
Winston-Salem, North Carolina

LONDON NIGHTFALL

I saw the shapes that stood upon the clouds;
And they were tiger-breasted, shot with light,
And all of them lifting long trumpets together,
Blew over the city for the night to come.
Down in the street we floundered in the slime;
Above, in endless files, gold angels came
And stood upon the clouds and blew their horns
For night.

Like a wet petal crumpled,
Twilight fell soddenly on the ancient city;
The 'buses lurched and groaned,
The shops put up their doors.
And skywards, far aloft,
The angels, vanishing, waved broad fans of gold,
Summoning the spirits of a thousand hills
To pour the thick night out upon the earth.

EXIT

Thus would I have it:
So should it be for me,
The scene of my departure.
Cliffs ringed with scarlet,
And the sea pounding
The pale brown sand
Mile after mile;

And then, afar off,
White on the horizon,
One ship with sails full-set
Passing slowly and serenely,
Like a proud burst of music,
To fortunate islands.

BLAKE

Blake saw
Angels in a London street;
God the Father on a hill,
Christ before a tavern door.
Blake saw
All these shapes and more.

Blake knew
Other men saw not as he;
So he tried to give his sight
To that beggarman, the world.
"You are mad,"
Was all the blind world said.

Blake died
Singing songs of praise to God.
"They are not mine," he told his wife,
"I may praise them, they are not mine."
Then he died,
And the world called Blake divine.

ADVENT

I have no more gold;
I spent it all on foolish songs.
Gold I cannot give to You.

Incense, too, I burned
To the great idols of the world;
I must come with empty hands.

Myrrh I lost
In that darker sepulchre
Where another Christ
Died for man in vain.

I can only give myself,
I have nothing left but this.
Naked I wait, naked I fall
Into Your Hands, Your Hands.

I HAD SCARCELY FALLEN ASLEEP

I had scarcely fallen asleep
Five minutes, but no more;
When I awoke there were the self-same walls,
The self-same polished floor,

The self-same night without;
And, between all these and me,

Acre on acre of pale unscented flowers,
The same eternity.

SPRING

At the first hour, it was as if one said, "Arise";
At the second hour, it was as if one said, "Go forth."
And the winter constellations that are like patient ox-eyes
Sank below the white horizon at the north.

At the third hour, it was as if one said, "I thirst";
At the fourth hour, all the earth was still.
Then the clouds suddenly swung over, stooped, and burst;
And the rain flooded valley, plain, and hill.

At the fifth hour, darkness took the throne;
At the sixth hour, the earth shook and the wind cried.
At the seventh hour, the hidden seed was sown;
At the eighth hour, it gave up the ghost and died.

At the ninth hour, they sealéd up the tomb;
And the earth was then silent for the space of three long
    hours.
But at the twelfth hour, a single lily from the gloom
Shot forth, and was followed by a whole host of flowers.

THE FUTURE

After ten thousand centuries have gone,
Man will ascend the last steep pass to know
That all the summits which he saw at dawn
Are shrouded deep in everlasting snow.

Below him, endless gloomy valleys, chill,
Will wreathe and whirl with fighting cloud, driven by the
    wind's sharp breath;
But, on the summit, wind and cloud will be still,
Only the sunlight, and death.

And staggering up to the brink of the gulf, man will look
    down
And painfully strive with weak sight to explore
The endless vales below which the long shadows drown.
Through every one of these he passed before.

Then since he has no further heights to scale,
And gods care not to witness that he came this way,
On the wind-bitten ice-cap, shaken by the gale,
He will watch the sunset fading of the world's last day.

And blazing stars will burst upon him there,
Dumb, as if heedless of his hope or pain,
Speeding no answer back to his last prayer,
And, if akin to him, akin in vain.

AUTUMN

She of the lagging feet, the lazy words,
The banisher of birds, has come into these woods;

Her eyes are dark beneath her coppery hair,
I see them glowering, flashing everywhere;

Over her head there hang dark bursting grapes
In heavy clusters, sharply sweet to taste;

Strayed from their towered city streets, wanderers will mark
    afar
Over the hills south-westward, the red banners of her war.

Down lamp-lit lanes'at twilight they return,
Where burn the house-fronts against sombre night.

Pools against banks of crimson will tell of her passing still,
And vivid asters flashing on the vermilion hill.

THE ENDURING

If the autumn ended
Ere the birds flew southward,
If in the cold with weary throats
They vainly strove to sing,
Winter would be eternal,
Leaf and bud and blossom

Would never once more riot
In the spring.

If remembrance ended
When life and love are gathered;
If there were none to think on us
Long after we had gone,
Song would not ring, nor voices
Talk at the doors in the evening:
Life would be barren and shattered,
Earth would be turned to stone.

But there will be autumn's bounty
Dropping upon our weariness;
There will be many sorrows
And joys to haunt us still,
There will be dawn and sunset
Though we have cast the world away,
And the leaves dancing
Over the hill.

THE ROCK

This rock, too, was a word:
A word of flame and force when that which hurled
The stars into their places in the night
First stirred.

And, in the summer's heat,
Lay not your hands on it, for while the iron hours beat

[118]

Grey anvils in the sky, it glows again
With unfulfilled desire.

Touch it not; let it stand
Ragged, forlorn, still staring at the land;
The dry blue chaos of mountains in the distance,
The slender blades of grass it shelters are
Its own dark thoughts of what is near and far:
Your thoughts are yours, too; naked let them stand.

SONG OF THE MODERNS

We more than others have the perfect right
To see the cities like flambeaux flare along the night.

We more than others have the right to cast away
Thought like a withered leaf, since it has served its day;

Since for this transient joy which not for long can burn
Within our hearts, we gave up in return

Ten thousand years of holy magic power
Drawn from the darkness to transcend death's hour.

For every witch that died an electric lamp shall flare,
For every wizard racked, the clear blue air

Shall roar with jazz-bands into listening ears;
For every alchemist who spent in vain his years

Seeking the stone of truth, a motor-horn
Shall scare the sheep that wander among the corn.

And there shall be no more the spirits of the deep,
Nor holy satyrs slumbering upon the steep,

Nor angels at a manger or a cross.
Life shall go on; to ugly gain or loss;

Yet vaster and more tragic, till at last
This present too shall make part of the past:—

Till all the joy and the tragedy that man knows
To-day, become stiff gravestones in long rows;

Till none dare look on the mountains ranked afar,
And think, "These are the cast-off leavings of some star."

THE PORTRAIT

Through his eye searching far
Over the bone-stretched rondure of my face,
Exploring every scar
And lingering on the meaning of each trace,

Through his hand searching to fulfil
The image left unmoving in a brain
By the packed cohorts of my thought and will
Externalized in flesh, I shall remain

Not mine but mine and his;
A link 'twixt thought and act none can discern.
Yet my portrait is this,
And in it all my days unspoken burn.

Yet only doubly unknown time may mark
What his hand wrought in colour, line, and tone;
And a space uttered outwardly of that dark
And changeless silence where life broods alone.

LATE SUMMER

Against the sky, a cloud-white bowl of flame,
The trees stand out, in masses of dark green;
Dizzy sunlight, fainting shadow,
To the distance dimly seen.

Great billows of haze rise up, slowly uncoil
Their heavy folds in silence. Underneath the leaves
The heat consumes the dew. A swallow darting
Skims, brushing the brown eaves.

Weedy gardens, rank, neglected, smoulder
With ragweed, thistle, purple and scarlet flowers:—
Like gipsy girls they are staring
Through eyes unquiet and sombre,
Down the long hollow silences of the hours:—

Seeking for something long ago vanished and forgotten,
Something that time has now taken away, and fate no more
  will bring;
The hour before the blossom of life fell and the apple of
  earth went rotten,
The passionate, shrill, riotous hour of the waking of the
  spring.

CRUCIFIXION OF THE SKYSCRAPER

Men took the skyscraper
And nailed it to the rock. Each nerve and vein
Were searched by iron hammers. Hour on hour,
The bolts were riveted tighter. Steel and stone
Did what they could to quench the fiery core
That blazed within. Till when the work was done,
Solid as a sepulchre, square-rooted to the rock,
The skyscraper, a well-polished tomb of hope,
Guarded by busy throngs of acolytes,
Shouldered aside the sun. Within its walls
Men laid a little gold.
                    But yet not dead
However long battered by furious life,
However buried under tons of frozen weight
That structure was. At night when crowds no more
Jostled its angles, but the weary streets
Of a worn planet stared out at the stars;
Its towering strength grown ghostly, pure, remote,

Lone on the velvety night in flights of gold
The tower rose. The skyscraper dripped light.

ISLE IRANIM

O mighty are the lights that shine above Isle Iranim;
Green, blue, and gold in clusters blazing,
They light the porphyry stairways, the colonnades, the towers.
The shipmen see them winking
Far off across the roaring foam-maned ocean;
And up upon the moonlit, tilting deck
They hoist in readiness their choicest bales.

O splendid are the flashing throngs that move about Isle
    Iranim;
Dark princesses in silken robes glide by,
Hunched bowmen and tall spearsmen haunt the stairs;
Above them scream the startled birds of night,
The dim moon wavers through the torchlit glare;
And multitudes subdued
By skirling music, bow themselves down to earth.

O drunken are the nights that roll above Isle Iranim;
From palace-courts there comes
Sound of the trumpeters and drums that hail king's revelry
    by night.
Men sprawl upon the flagstones of the streets;
Down in the harbour, ships deserted droop red straggling
    sails.

But, in the dawn, when with dark weary eyes
The revellers sleep heavily under smoked fizzling lamps,
Lonely, a fool shall stagger out upon the topmost terrace
    stairs,
And clutching at his painted cheeks, stare at the grey-green
    sky and weep.

BRAHMA

Brahma sleeps.
On his broad palm, the world,
Rose against blue,
A lotus-leaf
Silently shed, is curled.

Brahma dreams.
In the thick dull blur
Of his mind, unfathomed—
Fathomless ever—
Dreams stir and blur:
Worshipped and worshipper.

Brahma wakens,
Bids Shiva play;
Shiva dances,
Springs and dances;
The universe, time,
Man and his madness,
Sun, wheeling planets,
Sirius, Orion,

Worlds gleaming, perfect,
Woman's white shoulders,
Dust, worms and ruin—
All things to nothing
Are swept away.

BUDDHA AND CHRIST

'Mid Himalayan snow,
Where a mere step sufficed
Bare rocks at watch to show,
And darkly spread below
The world that humans know,
Buddha met Christ.

There Buddha sat him down;
Christ raised His hand on high,
Knitting His brows to a frown.
Buddha smiled; and the sky
Uttered a far-off cry.

Buddha's palm touched the earth;
Christ said: "I am Heaven's Son."
Buddha said: "Free from birth
And death is never one."
The sun-disk dipped, was gone.

Christ's tears flew down like hail,
Buddha's smile gleamed more bright.
Christ's brow was gashed and pale,

[125]

Buddha's third eye gave light.
About them closed the night.

Each might have gained some sense
Of one another's scope,
Buddha, moon-charmed, intense,
Christ snatching at heaven's cope.
But under, cold, immense,
Earth died: and vain was hope.

AN UNBELIEVER TO THE CHURCH

There was darkness over the earth till the ninth hour,
And then those watching heard a far-off cry:
"Eli Eli!" it said, and it had power
That seemed to split the solitude of sky:
It brought the darkness nearer. Stiff and high,
The temple veil was rent. King David's tower
Crashed down to dust. Men saw an eagle fly
Out of the silver flickering of a shower.

The hopelessness of that eternal Cross
Was far too great for human hearts to bear:
We must have easy balm for our despair,
Some soothing hope; not horror and sheer loss.
Humbling themselves and their immortal pride,
Men chose the barren stone where Peter's courage died.

WHITMAN

One does not quarry this mountain,
Armies alone can loosen these rocks,
Over the pits and the slag,
Foolish dark holes men have made,
Wave still the pines in mid-air,
Cataracts leap to the valley,
Deafening, shattering;
And the song
Of the loud wind through the woods,
Waking the birds in the spring, tearing free in the fall,
Hurtling away the shrivelled millions of leaves,
Is still heard
When the soul that upraised in his might
These naked slabs of nude stone
Walks now no mortal shore.

SONGS FOR ONE DEAD

I

Whether we cared for each other, and were happy, none can
   know,
Or whether we were parted, and parted had to die;
There is none that remembers, no one at all to show,
Time is as void of an answer as the noonday summer sky.

Yet it is written in a language that no living man has read,
It is spoken in a tongue that no human ear has known,

And it will be remembered long after I am dead,
When time and space have spent their last, and all worlds
    are overthrown.

II

The windows where we stood and thought as one,
See other faces now; and yonder where
Your garden slantingly faced the broad sun,
Others will walk and stare.

And feet will crunch the gravel to your door,
But not the feet that you heard pass that way.
I too must dive through earth's unbroken floor,
Ere I can find again one vanished day.

III

It is said the dead in their dark graves may not sleep
Unless they can hear, muttered above each head,
The sound of ancient prayers. I wonder why you keep
Such silence, being without prayers, yet dead.

Is there no strange fierce beauty in the earth,
No revelation from the ultimate sky,
To tell you of how little death is worth,
Unless you have earned the right never to die?

LAST JUDGMENT

There fell red rain of spears athwart the sky,
Flame flapped upon a heather-covered moor,
Green waves tossed high the ships that steamed near shore
And dashed their keels to wreck. Aloof and high

The evening star like a gold plummet fell
Into the shadowy horror of a sea
Frozen to glass. The sky split. Vacantly
Across the void there trailed the Snake of Hell.

Now out of every graveyard on the earth
There suddenly writhed in flame and stood up new as man
A being whose girth no human eye could span;
Two heads it had—one like a babe at birth,

The other like a skull. It hollowly spoke,
Like wind that roars in echoes huge and vast,
Against the unconceived, unfathomed past:—
"Now ended is God's high and pitiless joke."

PART FIVE

AUTOBIOGRAPHY

I. BEFORE AND AFTER

Iron cities swim upon the sea;
And tailored millions travel
Across lacustrine gravel:
Digging the foundations for an electric sign,
Men found a mammoth's tooth and a Roman bottle of wine.

Ten years, ten years,
Shall bring you many changes, and alter hopes to tears.

The horse has gone on into eternity:—
In our Hispano-Suizas, cushioned, soft,
We gaze aloft
Watching a winged thing cut across our sky.

The gondola is going;
The chug of motor-boats will rack those walls,
Explode across the halls
Once rocked to melody by the waves' soft flowing.

The negro thinks the missionary
Speaks with departed spirits upon the telephone;
So he has grown
No longer black and upright, but morose and wary.

New millionaires and movie-stars combine
To make a dumb show of the Vatican;
Tibet to Oshkosh is a short day's span;
The Dalai Lama asks an actress out to dine.

The white mob conquers the worn-out world to-day,
Before the hosts of yellow, black, and red;
Civilized, white, and barbarous we will stay,
Before we are to outer darkness shed.

As moving through music,
Repeating, rising, suffering, and crying;
Yet slowly and inevitably
And darkly dying;
I pause one breathless moment
To recollect my dreams;
Now all of them that mattered
Is long burnt out, it seems.

Kisses upon a hill-top
Where rhododendrons ran aflame
Against a wall of glittering leaves.
Cool through the twilight moved your fresh bright body,
Bringing me offerings of joy.
Beware of love's late fire;
From its black traces you will never part;
Your will has changed to water, your best flame to destroy.

There was a blaze of hopes that came to nothing;
And there was shining wine,

There was a city full of lights and voices,
And there was youth at play,
Swift as a dancer leaping
Through rain of roses over Tyrian marble,
To catch applause;
There was a blackened gibbous shape at midnight rising,
Of which no one—till later—knew the cause.

Ten years, ten years,
Will conquer youth and quell your hopes and fears.

Suddenly, with a laugh,
The Operator changed the scene;
Darkness fell on the Russian Ballet curtain—
Trains full of smoky soldiers sped on Paris—
I stood sagely regarding,
With thoughts grown grim and cold,
Midsummer snow.

Ten years, ten years,
Shall I have ever done with their unsummed arrears?
Or shall I approach rapidly,
Like a great ship with sails outflung,
But with its dark hull rotting beneath it,
Rotting and letting in the incoming sea,
The whirlpool wherein I collapse
At the latter end of the world?

Emerging with the daybreak,
Drifting in silence down a sluggish river,
Between two banks dividing
That held the summer in them, firm forever,
I saw the cottonwoods
Receding southwards,
The arms of the cypress
Touch the horizon;
The great white pelicans
Far off, beating and fluttering their outstretched wings.

At Cairo the ranks of the corn stood up—a plumed immortal
    army:—
We drifted on in a sunset of smoky heat:
There was a flatboat hanging alongside laden deep with
    melons,
A passion-flower vine upon a whitewashed wall.

At St. Louis we waited all morning with the roar of the
    trucks cutting across the cobbles;
The river running through the great arches of the bridge
    above us;
The mules flicking their ears against the flies.

At New Orleans we tied to the levee in the quiet of early
    morning,
We wakened to find the city washed clean by early daylight,
City once seen in midwinter glory, now drowsing in summer
    silence.

And the river took me,
The river which flowed through my dreams and which goes
  on still in my heart;
The masculine yellow Mississippi which the railroads had
  made forgotten,
The river of Spanish explorers, of canebrakes and floods, the
  pathway of war that had cut through the heart of my
  South.

I saw it once and I see it now forever,
For with the next spring
It was time to go
Back to grey Europe,
Shuddering under the war-cloud that hung loweringly
  poised above it.

Manhattan, the opulent and the daring, faded;
The broad-shaded Southern town that I loved went out of
  existence,
The deep jade of the redwoods about San Francisco, the fire
  of their orange trunks disappeared from life,
The stony hillsides of New England, the sparse white farm-
  houses followed.
The hard grey streets of Chicago stretching relentlessly forward into the prairie from the shores of the wide blue
  lake,
These could not keep me back.

There dropped upon them all the calm of a green-wooded
  harbour,
Terraced streets and belfry by the shore,

[137]

Skeleton clippers standing at attention
Amid a world at war.

III. THE SHIP GOES DOWN

Suddenly from the deck a proud still face,
Too far away to help, too old to dare,
Flashed; and it darkened as the ship went down,
On Europe never more to be the same.

There were guns, guns, guns pointing to me;
Guns ranked to east and west and north and south:
Between their muzzles I fled
Far out upon the snow,
Towards the summit dark amid the pines
Where none would ever follow.

Caught in the whirl, we drift
This side and that, to and fro, every way:
For some the darkness did not ever lift;
Did I win through that day?
In racking clamour, two years fled
To take their places with ten million dead.

But I upon a summit hid in mist
Wondered what could the future hide from view:—
A cross, a resurrection from the tomb,
Or merely nothingness?

A ship across the west drew breath and paused.
Sunset—orange and maroon—
Once more for me there was naught to do but go.

IV. THAT WHICH WAS LEFT

Flickering heat of an August morning,
Through which my heart laboured and pounded,
Like a dung-cart going over cobbles;
The pavements turning about me
As in a drunken dream.

He stood upon the platform and he saw
The mob assembled, sixty feet below,
The iron sides of the tank
Twelve feet across, the dish of shallow water
Into which he must plunge.
The wind was soft and easy.
Hushed and yet wonderingly the crowd attended.
He poised and raised his arms aloft
And then deliberately he turned his back
And toppled down.

His body cut the air;
Twice did he turn himself before he reached the bottom:
Two somersaults and you will find
Me—the resounding harp-like sea shut in its narrow shell,
Twelve feet across;
He struck into the water,

An instant later stood up dripping.
Few cared to clap their hands.

Still cutting through time's warp and weft,
The world, like a diver, falls;
The world is of its best bereft,
Best take unaltered what is left;
Heed you, whom darkness calls.

Dry year of eclipse—the summer labored on and on,
Like an old voice mumbling in a long-deserted room:
The slave yearned for new slavery—the free man despaired
    of the dawn.
At spring a million flowers enwreathed a forgotten tomb.

He went, the one in whose eyes I had trusted,
On whose breast I had leaned
As John leaned on Another's breast and heard the bread
Broken—the sound of loosing star from star.
Thrice did he come to me from the cold tomb,
Thrice I denied him after he departed.

And he with the grey eyes,
Writhing his lips into a bitterer smile
Of stern endurance of cold, joyless fate;
He too moved swiftly out of my life forever.
He left a song that moved in endless night,
The song of man, abandoned by his gods.

I heard it clearly on the barren moor,
Where the wind strikes amid the grass,

Immense and sunken monoliths of weatherbeaten stone;
The wind—it blows a tone
Of old impersonal things,
Which for our sorrow do not grow the lesser,
Though time goes by them on unchanging wings.

This that I heard made all that I have been
Like to a theatre in which scene on scene
Appears without an actor, and where no applause
Breaks forth; these fancies in the brain, what is their cause?

"Man did the gods make
Nature's sole master;
Broad-browed and lordly,
King of earth's harvests.
Many the gifts they gave to him;
Much joy he won therefrom.
He whom they abandon,
Exile from their glory.

"Weak, puling, foolish,
He strives to remember
His kingdom forgotten.
Pitiful, lonely
Last remnant of man!
With him shall the gods not reckon,
Neither length of days,
Nor lasting renown,
Nor love requited,
Shall be his."

After a year of rain old dreams came back,
And once more flourished, maybe darkly grew
Within a field unseen—if the last track
Back to that magic past I only knew!
Sometimes it seems in me; again in you.

Strive then no longer,
Waken or slumber,
Labor or suffer,
With your small day be content:
Yet be at peace within your inner mind,
And you will find
Far, far beyond your loneliness and pain
Grey memories ripening under heavy rain.

THE BLACK ROCK

(TO THOMAS HARDY)

I

Off the long headland, threshed about by round-backed
    breakers,
There is a black rock, standing high at the full tide;
Off the headland there is loneliness,
And the moaning of the ocean,
And the black rock standing alone.

In the orange wake of sunset,
When the winds have fallen silent,

And the shadows slip and meet together from the edges of
 the sea,
Settled down in the dark water,
Fragment of this earth abandoned,
Ragged and huge the black rock stands.

It is as if it listened,
Stood and listened very intently,
To the everlasting swish and boom and hiss of spray;
While afar off, to the westward,
Dark clouds silently are packed together,
With a dull red glow between.

It is listening, it is lonely;
For the sunlight
Showed it houses near the headland,
Distant trees and flowers;
For the sunlight caused to grow upon it blades of scanty
 grass
In the crannies of the granite
Here and there;
For the sunlight brought it back remembrance of a world
Long rejected
And long lost:
Showed it white sails near the coast,
Children laughing in the bay,
Signs of life and kinship with mankind
Long forgot.
Now the sunset leaves it there,
Bare, rejected, a black scrap of rock,

[143]

Battered by the tides,
Wallowing in the sea.

Bleak, adrift,
Shattered like a monstrous ship of stone
By the waters, on its voyage;
With no foot to touch its deck,
With no hand to stir its sails,
There it stands.

II

Gulls wheel near it in the sunlight,
White backs flash,
Grey wings eddy, curl, are lifted, swept away,
On a wave:
Gulls pass rapidly in the sunlight
Round about it.

But the black rock does not welcome them,
Knows by heart already all their cries;
Hears repeated for the millionth millionth time
All the bitterness of ocean
Spoken in their voices.

It still dreams of other things,
Of the cities and the fields,
And the lands near to the coast
Where the lonely grassy valleys
Filled with dun herds deeply browsing
Sweep in wide curves towards the sea:

It still holds the memory
Of the wild bees booming, murmuring
In the fields of thyme and clover,
And the shadows of broad trees
Towards noon:

It still lifts its huge scarred sides
Vainly, to the burning glare of noon,
With the memory of doom
Thick upon them;
And the hope that by some fate
It may come once more to be
Part of all the earth it had:

Freed from clamor of the waves,
From the broken planks and wreckage,
Drifting aimless, here and there,
With the tides;
Freed to share its life with earth,
And to be a dwelling place
For the outcast tribes of men
Once again.

III

In the morning,
When the dark clouds swirl swift over
From the southwest, dragging with them
Heavy curtains of grey rain,

The black rock rejoices.
All its little gullies drip with cool refreshing showers.
All its crannies, all its steeps,
All its meagre sheltered places
Fill with drip and tinkle of the rain.

But when afternoon amid the clouds
Leaves adrift cool patches of the sky,
Moving like smooth stretches of the sea
Between floes of polar snow;

Then the rock is all aflame;
Diamonds, emeralds, topazes,
Burn and shatter, till it seems
Like a garden filled with flowers.

Like a garden where the rapid wheeling lights
And brown shadows drift and sway and fall;
Spring and summer and red autumn chase each other
Moment after moment over its face.

So, till sunset
Lifts once more its lonely crimson torch
Menacing and mournful, far away;
Then an altar left abandoned, it stands facing all the horizon
Whence the light departs:

Massive black and crimson towers,
Cities carven by the winds from out the clouds of sunset
    look at it;

It has dreamed them, it has made this sacrifice,
Now it sees their rapid passing,
Soon it will be bleak and all alone.

IV

Abrupt and broken rock,
Black rock, awash in the midst of the waters,
Lonely, aloof, abandoned,
Impotent to change;

Storm clouds drift off,
The sun strikes the hills far inland,
But you are forever tragic and apart,
Forever battling with the sea;

Till the waves have ground you to dust,
Till the ages are accomplished,
Till you have relinquished the last reluctant fragment
To the gnawing teeth of the wave.

I know the force of your patience,
Have shared your grim silent struggle,
The mad dream you have and will not abandon,
To cover your strength with gay flowers.

Keel of the world, apart,
I have lived like you.

Some men are soil of the earth;
Their lives are like harvest fields,

[147]

Green in the spring, and gold in their season,
Then barren and mown;

But those whom my soul has loved
Are as barren rock standing off headlands,
Cherishing perhaps a few bitter wild flowers
That bloom in the granite year after year.

THAT DAY

That day
Was like a ruby crusted with brown mud;
A jewel hooped about with battered gold,
Wrenched from a crown and thrown
Amid a mob, loud-chaffering by a stall.
It was to them like any other day,
No eye had part in it, but we who saw
Ourselves torn free at last from space and time,
Kindled again to the old gleam of flame,
Within its heart that held our very souls
That day.

The rhododendrons blazed beneath the rain;
Crimson they flashed without against black hills
That day.
As, in the faded shadows of a room,
We sat and drank our wine.

You said,
"You should be glad of song even in this hell."

And truly I was glad
As an old tree, long shedding its last leaves
Rejoices, thinking of the sap it had.

The city kept our hearts in tune
That day:
Behind the green partitions broidered over
With an old faded pattern of pink-centred flowers,
There seemed to us to hover
A distant singing that went by for hours:
Voices were rising and falling
In the chanting of a mass;
Days staggering under dark regret may through my future
    pass,
But still I know for once there came a word
Not breathed by human lips, but in the heart's core heard.

Without, as at a show,
The crimson rhododendrons stood bowing in a row
Like princesses with quilted skirts of green
Purfled with crimson silk; the dry and lean
Shrill air of April scraped its loud gavotte
Against their boughs, that day.
The while, about that spot,
Rain-haunted ranges mingled black on grey.
Far off on foothills red-brown roof-tops glowed,
Lisping unquiet poplars lined the road,
But you with your pale lips alone could say
Wherefore I had to turn the other way.

That day
My life was tautened like the dark round bow
Of the grim wind when the dawn-archer comes
And loosens his arrow-flight of light against the stars;
All of my being, evil and good, prepared
To spend itself in one mad sacrifice,
That the new vision we both shunned and shared
Might safely rise.

But afterwards,
The ruby of the crown was tossed aside,
The singing in the distance all died down;
The rhododendrons shattered under rain;
The flame that lit the distant hillside town
Faded to brown.
When all that could be done was done,
When all that could be said was said,
Our wills were broken and shed
That day.

TO COLUMBUS

I

These were the seas that you knew, and these were the ways
        that you followed,
From your Genoa of the dark narrow streets, where the
        sails flapped against the fronts of the houses;
The wave of the Mediterranean, evenly spaced, foamless
        wave ever advancing and never returning,

This was the power that lured you on, and perhaps also the tale of some yellow-shawled Arab sailor

Whose dark brown sunken eyes burned strangely at you, kindling with vivid fire

Above his scarred and sunken cheeks, weathered by tropic tempest.

He spoke to you of Cathay and the way thither, from the ports that open on the red desert,

Of Travancore and of Ind, of Taprobane and of the valley of spices.

And your eyes were taken away from him as he spoke, they went seeking the far-off horizon,

Taut as the string of a violoncello played upon by the light; above it opal-fired clouds were gathered

Piled high like the mountain-tops of dark islands waiting for an eternal conquest.

This was the land that you loved, that you left, that you did not see again:

The land of the grey-green olives climbing the hills in high terraces, of the black cypresses following in procession like monks in cowls, of the umbrella pines soaring to the tops of the mountains.

You left it for a harsher land, for Spain of the Kings, sunburnt, grey, desolate, a land where for seven hundred years the ice-flame of the Cross had struggled with the soft moony splendours of Islam.

You left it for the opening to the unknown ocean where pink Jebel el Tarif glares at Africa opposite, couchant and yellow and sullen,

[151]

You left it for the purple-green Gulf Stream breaking about
    you in foam, for naked brown Indian girls strolling
    amid palms, for solitude, glory, and silence.

II

When you had abandoned the land's last horizon,
When you floated to tropic waters,
When the wave took you not knowing whither you would
    go, when the wind in your white sails was silent,
And you abode in the midst of the seas
Like a swimming flash floating at the centre of a great shell
    dyed with purple-blue colors,

Then to you pacing the tiny deck of your caravel, each dis-
    tant cloud grew a portent,
Each floating weed promised an island,
Each shifting sea-breeze came laden with perfume of flowers
    and spices,
And the sea-turtles swimming about you through the blue
    depths below raised ever your hopes for a landfall.

The birds flew hither and thither,
The yards on the tall masts were righted,
The breeze failed and slackened, the sea ran like a river,
    the wind was adverse,
The men greeted you with scowls or with smiles, there was
    thunder in the air every morning,
Each day brought a new world closer.

You sailed onward from death to life and back to death
    again a hundred times,
You trembled at the oncoming of darkness,
The sun shutting his gates of orange and rose before you
    with a clang as of breaking metal,
The men crossing themselves as the lantern was hoisted to
    the maintop;
And each sunrise found you pacing the deck all alone with
    pale face and sweat-darkened hair.

It was pride, pride of faith, that still there upbore you,
Pride in your Genoa the superb, pride of a steel blade tem-
    pered in Spanish fires of conquest;
You tore up the tottering Cross and you bore it,
You the new Christopher, over the streams of the ocean,
In your pride exulting at the sufferings of the dying man
    hanging upon it,
For in truth you were bearing the black sins of Europe to
    a land where no sin had yet been.

III

We who have struggled upon a longer, more desperate voy-
    age,
Who have battled with tempests of the inner soul and have
    felt our planks give way to the waves that attacked
    them,
Who have lifted up hands in mad mutiny against our
    own brothers, who have covered the earth with dark
    slaughter,

Who have slain many a blossoming hope, and poisoned the
    spring air with horror,
Who have fashioned ruins to take the place of men;
We yet have struggled onward and on
Dreaming of hope beyond human hope, of a knowledge be-
    yond human knowledge,
Of a desire beyond human desire,
When the temptation of the serpent shall be no more bit-
    ter, nor the deed of shame done in the darkness,
In the days when men shall hold the sun like a naked child
    close in his arms, and woman stand laughing beside
    him;
When awakening in the morning they shall be made one,
    nor conceal with cold darkness and horror
The desire of their souls upsurging through dust, desire to
    attain the last heaven;
Where there shall be naught that we shrink from, naught
    that we dare not courageously and faithfully achieve
    here,
Twain made one in ourselves, and through ourselves out-
    wards for others;
When the desire and despair of mankind shall be crowned
    with immortal white glory,
We know that on that great day to come you will rise again
    as a red star beckoning us on.

New worlds yet unconquered waken each day within us,
Youth cannot fully conquer, nor old age fully conquer,
We shall abandon our works to the passing of years, to the
    waves' teeth and the winds' cry,

Setting forth with full sail for an ocean unseen, burning
with zeal to achieve it:
Youth is the season for planning and dreaming, for hoping
and praying, for seeking:
Still to come is the season for achieving all that we have to
achieve and for passing beyond.

We from the seas that you found, and the ways that you
wandered,
From clamorous and sullen streets where the spirit is stifled
and vanquished,
From cities of sham and of greed, from energies shattered
and wasted,
From a flat barren shore where the wave in mad tides rushes
up the grey land to devour it,
Come to the quiet deep bays that you lost, to the soft-swell-
ing olive-grey hillsides,
Where the Cross for five centuries longer has hung bearing
its burden of sorrow;
And we bring with us the old seed ripened to a fruit, the
proud will grown bitter and silent,
The suffering become a garment, and the glory grown a
dark weapon;
Scarified through defeat we come hither and we stand before you now silent,
You who once guided us westward, here on this eastward
shore will now look down and understand.

THE OLIVE

From the grey rock, the grey flame;
From the slope swooning in sunlight,
Downward the olive-trees leap and they carry
Grey-lichened tangle of branches,
Thin-bodied drifts of pale flame.

On the grey rock, the grey shadow;
Leaf that the proud Greeks prized,
Sapless and leathery leaf,
Sage-green and silver, you hang
Changeless there, year upon year;
Symbol of life beyond hope,
Drawn from the rock-strewn slope
Of the brown mountains descending
In the face of the midwinter sun.

Round you the seasons will pass.
Violets, dark flame in the grass,
Asphodels, spiky and pale,
Poppy, red-crinkled with sleep,
Dry husks and seeds, then again
Windflowers waking the gardens.
Grey-lichened, gnarled, you aloft
Lean to the sun-burnished sky;
Heedless how often years pass,
Or seasons fade out into death;
While your dark, purple-skinned fruit
On its grey branch never fails.

Greeks ran and found not their goal.
Romans tramped on into dust,
Knights of the Cross saw you far
Mingling your ash with their banners—
Christ knelt beneath you and groaned,
Darkly an angel drew nigh
Holding a cup of pale moonlight:
Coldly it brimmed to His lips,
And your leaves hissed a reply.

FROM PORTOFINO POINT

(IN MEMORIAM FRIEDRICH NIETZSCHE)

I

Music of violins and of guitars
Rises up straight from the night,
Slow like great walls of deep flame;

Music of faint winds that whisper,
Rattling like thin drifts of hail
Through the pale olive trees;

Music of mountains that sweep
Purple-brown waves frozen high
Over the horizon-edge.

Music of blue gulf that summons
With slow placid waters soft-creeping
Man's ever passionate soul.

[157]

Softly the night ebbs—the ships
Lie asleep in calm harbours;
Rest after fortunate day.

Slowly a bell tolls and far
Cypresses fling up black shadows
Into the star-powdered sky.

Round the moon poised in its zenith,
Pregnant and calm in the stillness,
Ashen light shapes a great ring.

Everything turns and returns,
Empires have faded and ebbed,
Empires to life will return.

Man has gone down to the sea,
Like a great ship flying high
At his proud masthead a torch
Shedding its sparks through the darkness:

Man has sat lonely and still
On his cold peak of despair,
Watching the ebbing of night
Over the valleys of dawn,
Dreaming of pale stars that dance
Over the peaks before day.

All is a dream, is a dream;
Waking we dream, and asleep

Maybe through dreams we awake
Seeking some meaning unseen.

True to the earth we have been.
Far on our mountain-heights
Like to blind eagles we gazed
Into the eye of the sun,
Waiting the hero to be.

True to a sea-borne flame
Others have been, and they fared
Beaten by storms beyond help
On to their doom in the night.

Flame of the noon and the stone,
Flame of the ship and the gale,
Either is flame, and beyond
There is naught but the silence of night.

II

Music of noon-rippling waves
On this glassy blue gulf of the sea,
Like a great azure-paved floor
Whereon the sun walks, unchanging:—

Music of bird-song that breaks
From the brown curve of the shore,
Where the grey olives ride high,
Feathery soft smoke blown aloft:

[159]

Music of bells from the tower
Beating out noon where afar
Slim campanili dream hidden
Over towns quiet, asleep.

Silently, far to the south,
Tuscany sleeps, and the bay
With its brown leonine mountains
Maned with white snows at their peaks,
Fades into still afternoon.

Here on this slope there are trees;
Green and grey olives; below,
On the smooth glassy floor of the sea,
Like a butterfly floating and poised,
One ship with white sails outspread.

Man's life is like a lone ship;
Cold, unknown gulfs watch below;
Over his head still unchanged
Rushes the sun—at some hour
Marking the still height of noon.

Height beyond height—for no higher
Than his own noon can he grope,
This is man's tragedy.

Tragic height—now never more
Light can be shed; hour on hour
Going down, going down, loosing far

Flame from the empty horizon,
Kindling peaks soon to burn out,
Man must go on in the darkness.

Lonely is night but more sad
Is the flame of the noon, for it gives
All of its glow but in vain;
Poured out on the earth without ceasing,
Which takes it with never a thought.

Here one has paused and his power
Was as the sunlight that gives
Rays washed away by the night.

Here one has wandered and now
Still through the noon glides his thought,
Blazing on blue glassy floors,
Blown through grey olive trees,
Quivering up peak beyond peak,
With the power of a dream unfulfilled.

III

Mountains rest far in the noon,
Mountains are smoky and still;
Snow-avalanches have thundered
Down to their bases; they spread
Here where the valleys sink deep,
Split as with axes in earth.

Barren and gullied and hoar,
Haunt of the eagle scarce-seen,
Wrinkled and dull with their tops
In a hundred-mile circle round spread,
Mountains enkindle to life.

It is the still hour and I
Go once again to the mountains,
Bearing my ashes of hope
To the altar-like summit, most still.

Pale living presences, peaks,
Star-watchers, guardians of snows,
Be you my witness of song.

Be you the witness of flame;
That my darkness is ended, that night
Has taken its own; that I come
Lonely, my penitence shattered,
Back to unchanging glad day.

Be you the witness I seek
Poised far beyond human hope,
That the flame will soon pass when I go
Seaward as streams that leap down
Spurning the sheltering earth.

PART SIX

ELEGY ON A TRANSATLANTIC VOYAGE

I

Iron hammers clanked, and tilting furnaces poured
Rivers of molten steel to forge this shape;
Elliptical whale that pounds with steady beat
Snorting through high red funnels towards the sky:
Indifferent to the winds, it swings across
The wastes where Thetis and the Tritons mourned;
Shouldering aside the weed, the fog, the drift,
And the last solitude where man is lost.

And hollowed out within its dripping sides,
Long tilting corridors and dark narrow rooms;
Stairways and panelled halls where music plays and tables
Gleam with white napery and nodding flowers:
And halls where steel shafts gleam like polished dancers
Whirling their gleaming arms and heads on high
Beside the flame-banked rows of furnaces,
A city swinging between earth and sky;
Nation not marked by individual will
But by direction of the compass and
The drift of the world's dancing floor until
The shores shut in, and all in silence stand.

The mane of the wave breaks hissing
White, against utter blackness;
We stand beside the rail:
Brown furs about your throat,
Within your eyes a challenging light
That soon will pale.

We are dredged up and thrown together here in unending
    darkness,
Fools of the night's dark surge that knows no echo,
Held lonely, longing, careless here, awaiting coming dawn.
Your dove-grey eyes I see, your hand I hold one moment;
The helix, the propeller draws us on.

Soft languid sparks beside our keel burn out, they ebb and
    falter
Into the liquid furrow of our wake;
Who am I? Who are you? Soft eyes that rest on mine,
The moment is taken from us; ere we can fix, we falter;
Ere we can speak as one, the winds our words will take.

III

Slim feet move rhythmically across the floor
Swayed by the music's tide,
But loosed alike from thought and from a shore
These feet now glide:

And there, without,
As stunned by fog, the roaring animal bellows
That bears Europa on his back,
And threshes on, unheard;

Slim feet will glide, but weary feet will creep
Towards their cots; while I apart, in pain,
As lonely as the sea that knows no sleep,
Revolve an object, bitter thought, again.

IV

Not yet is Hesperus risen
From this wide sea; the sunlight
As focussed by the lens of sky about it,
Puts out the masthead lantern,
Alters the shape of motion,
Creates a silence where once speech has been.

The old seed, long ago,
Floated upon these waters;
It has divided now a million times,
Yet once again, closed in its husk of iron,
New lives within it start to sprout and grow.

V

As if created suddenly by a will we dared not speak,
Or rising to bound in our too free moving fears,
On the horizon motionless a blue beak
Of cape more solid than a cloud appears.

Between the yawning chasm of Broadway's foaming jaws,
Gleaming with glittering teeth up to the sky;
And Piccadilly's swirling current of dark flesh, the magnet
    draws
One slender thread of memory. It will lie

Where gulls wing heedless down an unspoken track,
Porpoises leap plumping through a green billow's roar,
Where lunging bows meet the comber's cold attack,
And wave-worn captains chart one weary voyage more.

ELEGY ON THE JEWISH PEOPLE

I

From the land without green leaf or shadow,
From the paths of the empty desert,
From year after year without rain, from day after day with-
    out coolness,
From hour after hour of the sun hanging still overhead
Like a great sword of bronze, grinding itself out on the still-
    ness;
Pulse after pulse of black flame;
From the blue nights,
When the stars beyond human hope look down and make
    deeper our longing,
Like a sea in which actions and thoughts forever keep fall-
    ing and falling;
From captivity, poverty, shame,

And slow patience sullenly burning
To endurance that cannot be altered, though wrecked in despair and desire,
You emerged, a strange flame of the spirit to beckon us on;
To light and to life,
Or to darkness and death,
Who knows—who can say?—
But to-day
The deserts have opened,
The deserts have yawned and have uttered a voice,
The deserts have spoken:—
"God is the thunderbolt that falls, when the heart otherwise
    would be broken."

You did not heed the ebb and flow of hopeless dreams;
You made bricks for the Egyptians for twice two hundred
    years;
You were the scourer of floors in Cyrus' palace hall.
Nation on nation took you captive,
You had neither kin nor honor nor hope nor home;
Byword of the earth, abject object of contempt and pity,
You clung on still to a hope you dared not understand.

You did right, O stubborn people, in rejecting Christ;
Christ could not save the world, there was still pain, violence, hunger,
Oppression in the name of the High God, iniquity, decay;
Death at the end of the road, death and defeat for each
    footstep;

You were the witness who could not yield; you waited for
  another verdict.

II

If you ask me to go with you a mile in the morning,
I will go with you twain;
But woe unto you if you seek to turn this to your advantage,
I will wipe off against you the very dust under my feet.

If you dare go seeking God, aflame with desire and longing,
I will seek side by side with you that vision never lost.
But woe unto you if you wish thereby to stand loftier than
  your fellows,
You will be cursed in the name of Him whose glory it is
  to be just.

III

The flame of the naked desire
Moving through darkness and daylight,
Like the beat of hot waves on the yellow sand where the
  stiff date-palms
Hang fructifying clusters,
Moves in my heart and the call
Of the slim pantherlike women
Pulls me, unpierced, to the shores:—

I will create one white flame,
I will consume my impurity to a fire that blackens the day-
  light;
Since my God will not answer

[170]

The longing I have, I will build what He cannot achieve.
In my barren self will I gain
The pure fulness of heaven;
I will mock with my inward-urged power the blue sky and
the empty brown earth.

IV

Rejoice, you far isles of the sea,
Rejoice, you forgotten great nations,
For he whom you longed for will spring,
No longer meek and bowed down
Nor bondsman, nor slave unto dust!
But conqueror in his own right:—
He will rise up in the morning
As a pure, naked, dark sword!

ELEGY ON LONDON

I

Out of a chaos of red chimney-pots,
Entangled with the rain, ten miles of rooftops scattered
Weaving thin meshes of flimsy smoke this humid autumn
morning,
Steeples of London surge up into the clouds,
Glittering windows catch vagrant gleams of sunlight,
Dreaming suburbs scatter their drab streets,
Giant hills to south and north surge up as half-seen ghosts.

Below, the brown river stretches with its bridge,
Which from before the dawn to after midnight is not silent;
And the iron roar of traffic,
Like water ceaselessly pouring,
Beats endlessly through my ears.
Tug-boats and barges litter up the stream,
Files of trucks, 'busses, motor-cars converge,
Surge over the bridge, are blotted out
By pale grey street-façades
Emerging from the mist like reefs beneath the sea.

City half-visioned, seen through endless haze,
Too vast your outward shape, too close your inner fibre,
Not as Italian cities to the South
You stand, where life like lava beats upon the stone;
Your life flows, stiff and secret,
Cringing, pathetic; yet you open wide
Mysterious, narrow, winding streets to take it;
And shape it to your strange, half-muffled song.

II

Over the infinite stir of human effort,
Over the waking war of the street traffic,
The steeples of London clash together
Their bells for noon;

Masses of cream-white cloud move through the depths above
    them;
Blackened by tattered smoke, the sky of late September

Bears them as wave crests on;
Under them, acres are darkened,
Sweeping of fuming shadows,
Cold surges over campanili, over these steepled towers.

Like sentinel angels weary and yet sad,
The slender snow-white steeples are tinged with the pale
    gold
Of the wan sunlight of September trickling down
Amorphous masses of smoke and sooty stone.

And round about their feet,
Millions of weak, magnificent souls are scattered;
Each one a wave that surges in retreat
Against the densely-clustering rock in vain.

III

Clamorous boom of bells,
Movement of tug-boats up and down the stream,
Faint flickering of ten million hopes
Across the pavements;

Vast hills to north and south
Shutting away the clean wind and bright sunlight;
Ant-heap of myriads buried in between,
Formidable effort undispersed, unscattered:—

Lonely and snowy steeples that still hold
The thought of something else, above the traffic,

[173]

Which scours on still beneath them;
Day after day, unchanged;

Magnificent vision under autumn skies,
When I am dead you will go on forever.

IV

Out of ten thousand dreams, this single instant;
Out of the unspoken love that bears us on,
Through years of hopeless hope, and hours of barren silence,
I made this dream for you who would not listen,
Who never will hear me till my song is gone;

Below, a slow red river,
Move still the 'busses, stream of life, with its dark need
To leave behind its highest hopes, its secret joys unspoken,
To find at last that sea where every hope is freed.

Still deep within my heart, fixed to my will,
Deep clang of bells, the cry that bids life stay
Not as a hurrying dance but proud and still,
Not for dark petty years, but only for this day:—

And still the clouds repeat,
Rolling like ocean-waves of dream above each sullen street,
That which is needless to wish otherwise,
Darkness and light contending for their prize.

Each in its turn will fade and fall apart,
Leaving behind in God's unseen, yet all-devouring heart,

Life smouldering still in tranced unconscious power;
Weaving grey veils of mystery between its eyes and light,
Though over every mystery, the stars still wait their hour.

THE JADE ELEGY

I

Golden blossom on the banks,
Crimson blossom in the leaves.
The grey mountain hangs like a mist in midair.

Golden parasols on the path,
Black hills against blue sky.
The grey mountain hangs like a ghost over all.

Golden blossom by grey banks,
Grey roofs amid green pines.
The grey mountain hangs like a tent in the sky.

Crimson blossom in the sky,
Yellow boats in the blue stream.
The grey mountain is washed in evening light.

II

Wide between the hills
Winds a yellow path;
In a yellow swarm
Rocks descend to it.

Starred with freakish pines,
Downward sweep green slopes,
And ascend anew
To another headland.

Through the round green gap
Lo, the hollow sea;
Like a deep blue jewel
Faceted with bays.

III

The gorge is deep; blue rocks and pines:
Above, where autumn storm-clouds go,
Tearing the mists to ravelled lines,
There is the snow.

On either side, steep mossy banks
Slope up into the sky to take
The coiling vapors of cloud-ranks,
And bring them down into a lake;

From whose chill brink a waterfall
Dashes downwards, day on day;
Striking the boulders in its fall,
Wetting the dark rocks with its spray.

IV

I cannot take this impulse from my blood;
I cannot take this image from my sight;

[176]

There rises through me, like an echoing flood,
The wild geese crying through the sky by night.

Alone, across the north,
In a V-shaped flight, at eventide they came:
The trees beneath them writhed their scarlet branches,
The earth breathed out its vast autumnal flame;

With necks outstretched to south,
With creaking pinions, with each harsh hoarse throat
Trumpeting the summons to that great jade mountain
That looms to seaward, under Fomalhaut,

Out of those swamps where winter, late in dying,
Spreads the brown sedge-grass for its winds to kill;
To those lagoons, where spring, eternal, sighing,
Grows her blue hyacinth—let him eat who will:—

Under the star-sown calm, or under tempest,
Under the rains that march across the plains,
Under the desert peaks or under thunder,
They still go forward:—and this thing remains:

I cannot take this impulse from my blood,
I cannot take this image from my sight;
There rises through me, like an echoing flood,
The wild geese crying through the sky by night.

The jade of the Emperor's hall is green;
The jade of the earth is smoky red;
But colorless is heaven's jade.

Should you seek for it in the mountains
It would still be hidden;
Stone axes have not digged it,
It closes round the thrust of tempered swords.

Pure, cold, and voiceless
It waits within the prisoning rock;
Hard is it as the way of birth and death,
And soft as soundless water.

The jade of the Emperor's hall is green;
The jade of the earth is smoky red;
But colorless is heaven's jade.

ELEGY AS EPITHALAMIUM

I

We were born in flame, and we go back to flame;
Whatever our hearts may ask, we have no right
To share God's lonely and unspoken name
But by descending downwards in the night;

That which is hid within enkindles breath;
And it is so, and will be ever so
Long as there lives what in the midst of death
Will balance all we know or cannot know.

Life will not come to us nor art make free,
Till in the circle of firm flesh we tread
Where two souls in immortal transciency
Meeting, unmeeting hourly, wed, unwed:—

It is the unpermitted lures us on
Through the permitted; and our single power
Is through the darkness to transcend the dawn
And by aspiring to annul each hour.

Love with a sword of light guards still the gate
Of tireless hope; that love will never fail,
Till no more separate we become what fate
Withholds from knowledge; each another's all;

We have resolved the riddle of old fire,
Spoken the word unheard in human speech;
And in an instant, out of dumb desire,
Breathed forth a flame of faith not held in time's grim reach.

II

Like a great golden cloud
In windless noonday when the blue sky burns,
Upon two hearts at rest
The gods descend.

[179]

In a slow even flight;
The ankles of the dawn,
The rosy breast of morn,
The cold blue veins of rain,
The rippling ocean of the darkling cloud,
Lightning-like arms,
The ash-strewn brow of death.

Into the temple, open, dark, and still,
Which has been sleeping underneath the heart
Of earth across which sunlight pours, they come.
Arches resound with song.

Music and laughter run through lonely hills,
The dawn comes scattering flowers;
Flame leaps athwart the forest;
The rain runs laughing from
The arrows of the westering sun.
Death smiles to see their play.

Roses are caught and lost,
Larkspurs are bartered for a smile,
Beyond blue lakes are hidden
Anemones of cream and gold,
Metal sunflowers tangle
With tossed delirious darkness of long hair.

Like a great golden cloud
Drawn up from earth at sunset when the weary
Field-laborers' shadows slant through smouldering trees,
Suddenly, the gods depart.

But the temple they abandoned
Displays, invaded by fresh-greening trees,
Rank after rank, carven in mute delight,
The gods, in human shapes.

III

Dante looked through old memories back to heaven;
Surrounded by swift tides of quiring flame,
He sank into a thought of two grey eyes
And the last meaning of a long-dead name.

It is because there is a language lost,
A word born out of days we cannot know,
That there is less in words to tell love's cost
Than in what lips or hands or eyes can show.

This is the wisdom that no century
Can age or any learning ever teach;
The surge of blood-tides that in human hearts
Day-sundered, brood in silence, each on each.

IV

With the sea ebbing,
Raging behind us still with its gold-crested wave tops,
We stand with faces lifted
To the swift-coming darkness.

We peer to eastward
Across the emptiness of fields abandoned;
They were once heavy with the grain of autumn,
Now they are dead.

We wait, we see
The smoky glories of the orange sunset,
The evening star, a trembling topaz hanging
To the last thread of light.

As Orpheus faltering,
Vainly through the grey shadows of the underworld,
Someday I'll have no strength to call you forth,
Shade that has merged with some far deeper shade.

But in new faces,
In songs and dreams unknown to us,
In some unsought-for longing,
Swept by the last grey wave whose crest is blackness,
We silently stretch out our hands to greet the dawning.

And we will find it, after bitter strife,
When in some other world than here and now,
Out of immortal rain-drenched sleep awakening,
The angel of life
With the bright morning-star will touch anew each brow.

ELEGY ON THOMAS ALVA EDISON

I

In the beginning, light
Varied with darkness in swift, steady alternation;
Over the surface of earth, the gift of sleep and renewal,
Rhythm of waking, steady drone of the day;
Earth made anew by the sun, the meaning of morning
Out of the sack of darkness, the purpose rekindled;
The fields lying clear, the fogs and dews of evening
Sending back herds to their stalls, bringing back ploughfarers
    walking away.

In the beginning, man
Lived as the sun lives, scattering afar through the jungle
Fires of his camps and his tents, the lore of his steadings,
The glimmer of fishing boats going slowly over the sea:
Man was the master of fire, and the night had no power
So long as his light lived, nor had the dusk purchase upon
    him;
The glimmer of torches still sped him on to his homeland,
The blaze on his hearth still warmed his heart with mystery.

But there was yet night and the stars, and the world going
    onward
Height beyond height through the sky, with the centuries
    falling
Before it like waves cut by a prow, there was yet rainstorm
    and tempest

Shattering the beacons, quenching the insolent fires.
There was yet sorrow and darkness. So man in his longing
Sitting on listlessly by his burnt-out campfire in the twilight,
Dreamed of the flaming ramparts of sky as no longer
 quenched by the sunset,
But brought near, tamed, and subdued utterly to his desire.

Now the centuries flow on and slacken,
Now the seasons are changed and are altered;
Now the lights gleam far out on the ocean that laps the
 dark edge of the world,
Now the vast bulk of the Gulf Stream cloud is shaken with
 cry of the sailors
Squaring the yards to the tempest, busying themselves with
 the tackling:
Now the faint light from the shore answers the light from
 the masthead,
Now the new world at last rekindles the old world's fire.

And the night is new-conquered;
The unseen made seen, the cities made bright with men's
 longing,
Blazing afar to the sky, and written in long lines of street
 lamps,
Racing away, ranked sentinels, far to the distance;
Words travel under the streets, the whole earth is shaken
With babble of minute low sounds: the fires of the night
 stand unguarded.
Hands need not heap the billets here a little higher,
Hearts need not shake in a spasm at the ebbing of the fire.

In this frail glass-blown frame
The coil of filament still burns and glows:
Enkindled by a power that no one knows,
Spun from the whirring strength of dynamos,
And tamed to human use by man's creative brain.

To this thin wisp of thread
The world is debtor, and the crowning skies,
With their unnumbered galaxies,
Show less of marvel or surprise
Than this strange globe, whose spirit now is shed

Far into hollow night,
Through the last thicket piercing, and the great
Depths of the Gobi or Sahara, straight
To where the kings of old keep solemn state
On their stone thrones, upright.

But not within,
The light may press, not into heart of man
May the gleam go, not into the small span
Between the reason and the will; that gulf
Yawns deeper than it did when time began;
Dark with the lust for blood, haunted by hopeless sin.

And swifter now
The lights go out, and once again we see
Like islands rising in the midst of storms the dreams of man

Lashed by the waves of fate, arise and reassume
Their ancient majesty.

And still more swift
The years fly on in fear like stormbirds in the night;
Battling against a cloud they cannot lift,
Shaking the roots of being in their flight,
Desperately crying against coming night.

And in this world
Richer by far than any world yet known,
Man, like a haunted madman, takes his throne,
And tears off gilt and velvet, and flings down
Their fragments in the mud; he streaks with his life-blood
Great walls of gold and marble, one by one.

III

So to this grave we go, not seeking here
If well done is well ended nor if light
From other worlds dawned glimmering on that sight
That ebbed as leaves of autumn fell through sheer
Alleys of woodlands; we ask not if night
Could bring us further miracles to make clear

Us to ourselves. So through the raging storm
Breaking about our heads and breaking down
The proud shapes of man's spirit, one by one,
Justice and love and charity brought to harm,
So we are turning back to our last home.

There where one life-stream ebbed and the slow track
Of the coffin-bearers passed, carrying the weight
Of a long life that broke
Under the piled-up weight of age and fate;

There we turn back,
And scatter flowers, and think the things we do
Might somehow please this great dead man of ours
Who labored late and long and was in new
Ways worthy and faithful; but no powers
Could ever bring back souls from whence they flew.

The world without may dream on him, but none
On earth but he himself could make his being known;

And there is not one living in that land
Unseen, that heart or tongue could ever understand.

ELEGY ON THE BUILDING OF THE
WASHINGTON BRIDGE

Theorem made of steel,
Linking earth, water, sky,
In poised self-organized appeal,
Amid the droning myriads that daily strive and die;

Casting back still on time
The memory of that face
That out of thickets peered, where once did climb
The wild grape-cables twining in this place

From tree to tree in air
Aerial hammocks, until Hudson drew
His men to them and could their strength declare;
Him and his mutinous crew

Now time has whelmed: from towers that steeper are
Than ancient Babel's, now the appalling weight
Of grey steel tentacles you stretch out afar
To the opposing shore, to bear a human freight.

Night's gulf beneath you span
With outflung gesture, dwarfing by your scale
Nature by the titanic schemes of man
Who crawls along you, puny wisp and frail;

Nor could the gods disdain
To own you if their will be, ere time close,
To guide across the void our feet that pain
Up through the darkness, seeking what none knows:—

Some superhuman law
Fluctuant as water, flexible as wind;
Poised as an ark of awe
Above the flood, to justify mankind;

One road 'twixt thought and dream,
Will and desire, free effort and fixed power;
Fire frozen to a force beyond fire's gleam;
Through man transcending yet man's mortal hour.

Therefore not lightly I
Who marvelling have marked your towers soar
From the horizon of a full-charged sky
Of hope and fear, would speak one word the more:

That we may hold you not
As emblem of our grasping and our greed,
But rather as pure symbol of our lot:
There is a bridge before us we have need

To build; a bridge whose links
Are consciousness, whose roadway faith, whose anchoring
    towers
Are the flesh acting and the mind that thinks.
This bridge is not so easily made ours.

Since long ago were laid
Its first stones, ere man's annals 'gan to run;
And its last length is stayed
Here in a world made every day more one.

Unless by knowledge fire-tried and freed
The mutterings of the savage and that mind
That scaled this steel equation fuse in a human creed,
Then there is no bridge standing: vast and blind,

Cables like arms stretch gauntly through the air,
From nothingness to naught; till as the last days run,
We hurl ourselves from them into the last despair:
Knowing we shall not consummate the bridge 'twixt night
    and sun.

Then this vain thing we schemed and strove to build,
Girder and stanchion, bolt and strut and brace,
Must rest, a black abortion unfulfilled,
To shortly take authentically its place

Where under the sunset bleeding, mad with fear,
The river blares its death-cry to the night;
And the sky's green eye stares frozen still where sheer
Black cables dredge the twinkling shoals of light.

ELEGY ON AN EMPTY SKYSCRAPER

I

Against the wall of this sky,
Leaden pall threaded with cardboard boxes, the pale light
    of the towers
Flickers unearthly still,
Long leaden streets between them:
Against the wall of this sky, the cream-white faces
Of stone blocks bound in glittering steel gleam high;
Jut to the sky, and break
Packed huddled ranks of clouds and roofs apart
Thrusting their own horizon yet a little higher.

Beauty is spread
Here over hollow voids; beneath these walls,
Clamor of traffic slides through corridors,
Long elevator-shafts shoot mountainously downwards.

Steel on the surface repels
This drizzling daylight; through the inner core
Vertical darkness spreads,
Extends its empire upwards,
Forces the tower to tremble with dull sound.

Noise of wheels tuned to wheels
Driving the darkness skyward,
Forcing the human darkness that should hide
The earth in fruitfulness, still bleakly upward;
In a stark affirmation,
Stone flanged to steel here to repel the daylight;
Void affirmation, since the sky goes higher
And men drift past, unseeing,
Bowed deeper by the weight of locked-in stone:—

Balancing bodies against the heat that holds
Its swift course vertically downwards;
Dragging their heavy feet into its molten pavements,
Swaying their shrinking flesh against its reverberant walls;
Noise of wheels tuned to wheels,
Bewildered by the men that move amid them;
While still the tower lurches
Upwards with its long shadow,
Flight of white-ripples four-square on the sky.

Here in this drift against the wall of sky,
Steel arms that lift,
Tackle that rattles,
Torches that sputter,

Chattering hammers that shake the empty brain,
The roar and the mutter
Of the swift elevated train;
And the ships at the dockside,
The pencilled lines of the bridges,
The dull green carpet of park,
The wide grey floor of the bay—
Is all this living to-day?
The fuming and looping line of the surly river to westward,
Stained by the sunset to red—
Is all this living or dead?
Dead are the twinkling lights and the sombre reflections
Of the earth-dwellers stretched heavenwards here from
    below?
Who is there living to know?
Only the wide hollow offices, the corridors empty of light,
Tier after tier going downwards here into the night.

II

Thick pencil of shadow stretched across the street,
If I could lift
Your weight and make you write;
Or if at night
I could make move that fixed and arrogant light
That stands there emptily glaring to repeat,
In higher guise, the street-lamp's signal-flight;
What against all the words that we repeat
In vain to-day,
What is the one word I would make you say?

[192]

"Here where once stared in dumb hope to the sky
Man by his naked blaze, and saw smoke take away
In folds of undulating grey
His prayer, not knowing walls however high:
Here wall on wall is heaped, steel thread to thread
Is riveted to extend the ever-dead:
Vain flight of shadow where the chasms cry."

Is this the word, or is some other thing
That which I seek? The sky gives no reply;
Will man grow wise and grow another wing
As powerful as the one that set on high
This thing?
I do not know:
But slow the darkness gathers; echoes bring
Only the wild cries of mechanic woe.

III

Could I but strip you down,
Tear steel from steel in long peeled strips, and break
The interlocking blocks of cream-white stone,
Send them like autumn leaves swift spinning down,
Or level, near and far,
This city, spread about you greening fields,
Leave you alone, all empty as you are,
Gleaming-nerved flower that no grass reveals,

Either I'd do:
But it is vain within your walls to go,

[193]

To feel in your dead heart the beat and strain
Of hopes grown panic-smitten, to and fro
Millions of meaningless lights,
When all about you is the soundless night's.

There is wide space between
Man's topmast and his keel, and in it death
Comes without sign or sound or stir of breath.
No one shall fill that room, or take his place
In it, as stowaway or come-aboard;
Nor shall the meagre window-blind be lowered,
Nor shall the dark be levelled by a face.

ELEGY ON NAPOLEON

"My name means: the Lion of the Desert."

I

From the black sagging cloud
Heavy with thunder, brooding over the ocean,
The wind pours and its voice
Is as a human cry.

The waves attack the rock;
The lightning flashes: there against the granite,
With pale white face uplifted,
A weary frail man stands.

With naught but a human brain
To pit against the tempest;

The desire of a human heart
To match the desolate sky:

Alone and frail he broods
Under the stormcloud; and he sees how earth
Grows greener for each tumult of destruction
Loosed on the multitude from that dark breast.

And the cry of the sea-tempest
Rising in wrath, has grown to him a trumpet
Summoning his soul to blaze
As a fierce comet, fiery over earth.

II

The storm of the night dies down,
Shattering the pine-trees, rattling the steaming windows;
Lazily over the last cloud-rack
Stands the blue morning star.

Out of the East there rises,
Quietly, solemnly, slowly,
From golden domes of ruined, empty temples,
From sleepy old bazaars, from crumbling minarets,
From grey wastes where the jackal vanishes,
From the cold lairs of the brown secret jungle,
Out of the gold and turquoise heart of dawn,
Processionals of mists across the plain,—

Trappings and plumage of scarlet,
Prince after prince advances;
The wind is rolling elephantine clouds
Down the huge corridors of bald blue mountains;
Black bowmen release arrow-shafts of hail,
To the tune of a fluted singing:
And, in the midst of these,
Surrounded by a phalanx of bright spears,
His brows bound with gold rays, and filleted in scarlet,
Alone on an ivory chariot,
Drawn by two milk-white stallions foaled within the desert,
Great Alexander rides, the offspring of the sun.

It is as if the clouds were opening slowly,
Rank behind rank, wide-swinging gates of gold,
And in between them, fire-crowned, an eagle
Hovered within the burning empty sky.

He lifts his hand, the vision vanishes,
The morning star has gone behind the cloud-rack;
Like a dim figure struggling in an ocean
Of shouting, hoarse and greedy voices
He sees himself, wrecked on an iron lee-shore.
And round about, with stony visages,
Vulturine-beaked, the ancient rotting kings
Perch on their thrones, propped up with moneybags,
And stare at him with cold and fishy eyes.

Who can describe the furnace heart of man,
When will and suffering meet in endless conflict?
Who measures out the rhythm of mad hearts
Whose steady tread strikes hammers upon earth?

Through blazing day and drowsy starry night
Fires drift and dance and twinkle over hills.
Stone walls re-echo to a shouted name,
Which holds one dark wish hidden in its heart.

Armies melt under him;
Yet the great sphinx still watches and her claws
Twitch not, though on her lips
There curls in hovering mockery a smile.

Struggle of death and night
Encompasses him; red flecks upon the snow;
And ravens cawing
Over cold corpses, sprawled out upon darkness.

Fiercely the flame outpours,
And scatters desolation in its path;
Great towers enkindle, surge in smoke, and fall.
Dim figures scurry across ice-glazed rivers.

He who dared match his puny might
Against time's slow and dreary trituration
Of earth's old coils of pain, extending space,
Lies shattered at the last.

From the black sagging cloud,
Heavy with thunder, brooding over the ocean,
The wind roars and its voice
Is as a wild beast's cry.

Afar off in the track
Of the red sunset brimming over the ocean
A man stands and his face
Is a pale mask of pain.

He watches the swelling tempest
Gather for its last onset,
And on his forehead is written the proud answer:
Death.

Death in captivity,
Death bound about with iron chains to his rock;
Death in the storm, death without change or conquest,
No sword to lift,
No voice to hurry to his cry.

He for whom millions made
Their pact with death, because of his name written
Upon their hearts, and his face looking on,
While his voice spoke to their loud-beating hearts:

With his star blazing over,
His new will quickening lagging feet,

His brain resharpening their sword-blades,
Crownless now, finds his secret throne at last.

He is now but a mask of marble flesh,
A veiled light in a dark shrine where is silence.
A pinch or two of lost brown human dust
Which whirls about the earth, beyond decay:

And he lies cold and silent;
Shattered and beautiful, while the tropic storm
That beat its blue drum once more for his passing
Over the ocean, sullenly ebbs away.

v

The darkness of the gods that gazed upon him,
Too deeply now enshrouds our minds and eyesight;
We dare not grope to find
Even the meaning of a little hour:

Was it their will or ours
That drew this flame out of the stagnant deeps;
To fling it backward into the darkness,
We do not clearly know.

Red glares encircle the horizon of our hell,
And, in between, we flounder in the darkness;
Crowns, crosses, Caesars, crumble into dust,
And we with feeble eyes look forth and see

The momentary glimmer of a face
Pure, cold, and godlike, bearing for these who suffer
The image of a destiny that failed
Against the slow attrition of the dust.

ELEGY ON THE RUSSIAN REVOLUTION

I

Darkness broods over the East,
Over the plain, the land of horses;
Darkness and wintry silence,
And death.

But a blue-white light from north
Suddenly flares up at midnight;
And in the glare, on the horizon,
A horseman rides alone.

He sits on his great white horse,
A strong white bow is in his hands;
Beneath his gold-horned helmet
Thick braids of golden hair descend.

He goes forth conquering and to conquer,
He goes forth seeking a golden crown,
From the frozen marshes of the north,
To where the rivers bend southeastward.

A brood of lions follow him,
Shaggy-haired, with broad golden manes,
Eaters of sheep,
Founders of cities.

In the depths of the steppe,
Upon the banks of broad golden rivers,
Facing southeastward
The cities rise:

Kiev with its golden domes
On which there stands the cross;
Vladimir, Ryazan, Tver,
Novgorod, Moscow.

Lord Novgorod the Great
Looks to the north and east;
Moscow sits in the centre
And dreams.

The heroes go forth every morning
To battle with each other,
At night about the wine-board
They sit, feasting.

II

Out of the East
Comes the great dawn;
Red is the dawn,
Red and fearful.

[201]

From the southeast
Runs a red horse;
Foam drips from his bridle-bits;
His hoof withers the grass.

Dark is the man
Who rides on him,
Clad in black armour,
Lean and yellow his face.

He carries a great black sword,
With which to smite the people.
He has power to take peace from the earth,
That men may kill each other.

Under the yoke
The princes pass;
They are his oxen,
He their lord.

Every day in his mills
The grain is ground;
Every day rich tribute
Goes to the Golden Horde.

Down at Sarai
Is the camp of the Khan;
Wearily travel
The oxen thither;

Down at Sarai
The great Khan sleeps.
But the claws of his falcons
Are fastened into the lion's throat.

III

Noonday within the East,
Noonday and a great sound of bells,
Pealing and crying
That the Third Rome is born.

Out of the great red gates
Of the Third Rome
Rides a man in scarlet
Mounted upon a black horse;

A golden cross is on his breast,
A pair of scales is in his hand,
With which to measure out the earth,
With which to weigh the people's grain.

A measure of wheat for a penny,
And three measures of barley for a penny,
See that thou hurt not oil or wine,
See that the land is tilled.

But woe to thee, city of Pskov,
Woe to thee, Lord Novgorod!
The weight of the law of the Third Rome
Shall break your liberty.

Woe to thee, people of Rus,
Who set at nought the scales of law:
North, east, south, west, you shall wander,
But never find a home.

IV

Darkness broods over the East,
Over the plain, the land of horses;
Darkness and wintry silence
And death.

Far away to the west,
Hangs a great crimson fire;
It is the sunlight departing
Over the plain.

Out of the west there rides
The horseman of the twilight,
The great pale horseman
Whose name is Death.

And he carries in his hand
A lash of thongs;
And he has power to slay
With hunger;

And the eagles of the west
Pass after him.
Sea-eagles unsated
Fan with their dark wings his face.

Darkness settles faster
Upon the plain;
But the man on the great grey horse
Rides on.

On to the north,
Where a blue-white light faintly glimmers
Over the bleak pine forests,
Over the frozen seas.

Two cities have long ago fallen,
But there is one city to found yet;
A city of dreary phantoms,
A city of death.

At the edges of the north,
At the borders of the locked sea,
The pale horse rears
And stands.

Darkness, total darkness,
And in the darkness
Furiously, from east to west,
The winds go forth to battle.

v

But the souls of those who were slain
And buried beneath the granite,
Rise up again at midnight
And cry their final cry:—

"How long, how long the darkness,
How long wilt not avenge us?
For here our blood is written
On every inch of soil;

"For here our cause is crushed
Under the hoofs of proud horsemen;
For here our cause is forgotten,
Dead in the utter darkness."

So they cry out together,
And only the silence answers.
But the power of that silence
Has given them power to live:

And they go out to the streets of the city,
To speak to all hearts at midnight,
How the last seal will be loosened,
The final trumpet blown.

VI

Dawn comes out of the East,
Dawn with a tumult of flying horses;
White clouds of spring
Careering, galloping.

Stallion on stallion charging
Westward, to the horizon;
And in the midst of them
Rides liberty, unbound.

[206]

Her tossing golden hair
Is mingled with the sea of manes;
Her voice cries, "On, you wild ones,
Stop not nor falter!"

Out of ten thousand cities
A million weary eyes
Shall see her pass across the plains,
And cry, "Come faster!"

A million starving ones
Shall smile at her,
Shall stretch out their cold hands to her
Before they die.

A million broken ones
Shall make their bodies
The pathway for her feet;

A million eager ones
Shall leap forth from their trenches
To follow her command.

Like a white flame that gathers force,
She shall fill all the land
With song of victory;

Like the great flame of noon,
She shall spread out her wings;
And grant us all we longed for, could not find,
The peace surpassing human understanding:—

The light that rises from the blackened earth,
The great renewal of the coming spring,
The sword that shears the dreary clouds apart,
The joy that burns upon the new-forged sword.

ELEGY ON TINTERN ABBEY

That "Something far more deeply interfused
Whose dwelling is the light of setting suns"
Has changed direction now. And that which woke
In one man's vision, fired by the setting sun
Of faith from these old altars, has gone down
Like life-blood trickling from the wounds of Christ
Slowly, to the dumb grass. And that which stirred
Within the silence of the cemetery
That followed after the proud challenge pealed
From lips that loved America and France,
Was a loud mocking hoot from factories
Crying, "Come out; be filled." And so the world
Turned backward from its path and followed gold's
False rushlight gleaming from the dismal swamp,
Mocking the prophets always and their creed.

And thus the music of humanity,
"Of ample power to chasten and subdue,"
That still sad music breathed from out these stones,
Was lost amidst the mounting shriek and blare
Of "sell quick and buy cheap." And so the world
Grew one vast Manchester of laisser-faire,

Low and victorious, 'mong which stranger-folk
Who clinked the spurs of Cavaliers, or swore
The oaths of the mad Puritans, went down
To drink the stream of Lethe with their peers.

God of the world, Who suffers the unjust,
Poured out His potent spell. It fumed like wine
In many brains. One merely spelled out words
In some newspaper, and the morning's sun
Rose clear to greet them. Long as outward white
Was inward black, one was content to swear
That all was well with earth. Meanwhile the wheels
Turned furious, and the little wheels of Time
Beside them saw they ran the faster as
New nations learned the trick to make them turn.

No one can say what happened then, nor how.
Men had no time to pause and gather thought.
Earth in its furious dance spun one mad twirl,
And then beyond the wheels were sudden come
The lean grey throats of guns uneasily crouching
And searching skies for prey. What made the world
Grow dark, and then the awful echoes start,
Rebounding here and echoing there, none knew;
Only the wheels had got at last their way,
Not three hours then, but four years Calvary.

Meantime the dawn kept to its "priestlike task"
Of waking worlds too brutalized to ask,
Aught but "how long?", too agonized to know

Aught but the need of fitting on anew
One's gas-mask, fixing bayonets again
Against attacks unseen. To such a strain
As this now blew "the misty mountain-winds"
That once spoke liberty. And to this came
Songs of man's triumph in the swelling main
Full-tide set towards progress. Till at last
The sullen guns grew weary riddling earth
To rubbish-heaps and so withdrew again,
Leaving the beaten folk to cower there,
Behind the barrier of an empty word.

And then men saw, as dawn at last released
The last long trenchline furrowing earth defiled,
That man was fastened hand and foot alike
To his machines; not as Prometheus now
Chained to his sad rock and yet nobler than
The god that doomed him: but Ixion cursed,
Who raped great Hera, and hence, self-condemned,
Must roll through Hell forever on his wheel.

What then can free our fingers or dispel
The chill delusion of dark crawling thoughts
That haunt too close the tomb? Can madness save
The sanity of the void? Is there a tune
Not torn from man's guts by the fiddling bow
Of greed and ignorance hired each day anew
To play on them? Well, if there is, not here
May it be found, where, as a numbing spell,
Some ancient acquiescence haunts the dust;

But rather where the shells and shards are piled,
Vain effort, with the souls that strove in vain;
There you may find some outcast sons of men
Who see, but will not yield to their despair.

ELEGY ON THE LAST JUDGMENT

I

Men shall go on nor heed the signs of old;
The trumpets of the wind blow loud or soft,
The skies flare red and crimson; up aloft,
The stars like flocks still wander from God's fold:

The cities rise, and turn again to grass;
Their hungry hosts go seeking to devour
The ecstasy of one swift-ebbing hour:
So days will alter, swift to change and pass.

Wisdom unheeded still will speak or rave,
While thousands bound to selfhood will yet strain
Their bonds a little tighter, and again
Dry eager hands will rifle wisdom's grave.

The victory shall rest upon the lost,
The banners of earth's conquerors shall bear
A darkening stain; and slowly through despair,
Music shall speak its message to the crossed.

[211]

SALEM COLLEGE LIBRARY
Winston-Salem, North Carolina

The rivers roll afar to reach the south,
The winds run as they list, and blown along
The wharves of time, there drifts a tiny song,
In memory heard. Dust stopped the singer's mouth.

II

The rich man rolls along the crowded street,
The beggar at the corner spreads his hands
Out for a penny. Eager lovers meet:
A hearse goes by, and still the great world stands,

Stands as it stood, with whirling drifts of smoke
About its rooftops and, when spring arrives,
Green waves starred with long blossom that will cloak
The stark bleak branches of our wintry lives;

A child plays on the pavement. An old man
Goes slowly tottering past. Behind a pane,
A face looks out too scatter-brained to scan
The meaning of this world that moves again!

A priest upholds the consecrated host;
In a dark room one presses to his ear
The barrel, pulls the trigger. Through the lost
Drift and dark rumble, words come loud and clear.

They slip back to the past. The soldiers go
Marching along. Men mark them. Drunkards reel,
Whores sell a kiss. A thousand years ago,
Men were the same and felt even as we feel.

Each is alone. Shipwrecked at last in space,
Clutching with crippled hands, we strive to cling
One moment more to time's bleak rocky face,
Till we are beaten off by some dark wing,

And breathe no longer. This at last we know,
Lost to all but ourselves, yet striving to transcend
Ourselves, we go, or, dying, cease to go
Under the trumpet's menace to the end.

III

Smoke-purple lilac bursts and soars:
Now in the sky the swallow talks:
The leaves go shouldering upwards on their stalks:
Now through the streets the sense of out-of-doors

Runs like a dancer spangled in bright green
For some few days or weeks, but sure as breath
Is brief, it brings with it the second death,
Which does not smite the body, moves unseen:

Like a great cloud in which the thunder lurks
Cutting off leaf from leaf and flower from flower,
So that no other dream, no other power,
Comes back the same nor works as that one works.

For as the body slackens and decays,
Earth in its long death-agony turns from flame
To sparks and ash that kindles flame again
In stranger-visaged and far-wandering days;

[213]

Coming with skin of goats or fell of sheep
From islands where no ship moves, where no tongue
Of man is heard; where only time is strong
To bring the gift of suffering and of sleep.

ELEGY FOR ALL THE DEAD
1914-1918

And as our hearts march slowly to the dark,
The richer will their kingdoms be, made fair
By all our hopeless tears, and all those flowers
Piled on the mounds to rot in wintry air;
And as we slowly change, and strain our eyes
Yearning that we might see them, they whose feet
Are bound, whose eyes see the dark heart of God,
Will gain a world they ask not to repeat.

What can they do with it? What will be theirs,
They who are dumb at presence of such powers
As rigidly fixes jaws, as makes their eyes
Open and staring at a world not ours?
Why should we waste our grief? Why should we give
Them something of our own, a marble stone
To carry, and a wreath about their necks,
To bear through broken centuries alone?
And prayers and tears; why should we offer these
That which they need not, now they are utterly free?
A selfish load to lade these backs, so frail,
Making in vain for them death's final mystery.

Yet they will feed on such, and it will rouse
Their hearts long stilled below the earth's dull crust
Till they beat furiously, and they will go
Out from the grave, out from death's narrow house,
Not since they seek it, only because they must,
Towards some new world not yet shaped from dust,
A world not even dreamed, a world not ours.
And wandering weary millions of miles across
The desert of the stars, sown with strange fires,
They will make out of flowers and hopes and dreams
That which we found not, shaping from dead desires
A world we neither knew, nor dared to know,
A world of fiercer thoughts, more fiery dreams,
Beating and thundering through the walls of flesh:—
Rainbow-hued mountains linking earth with streams
Commingled of green ice and lightning-flash:
To daunt the unending darkness of that God
Whereby our feeble hopes are washed away;
They will be great with the greatness which the clod
Received but carried not. Its force must play
A part in spheres remote which we dare not
Achieve here for an instant. They will burn
With fury of our hearts poured out in vain
And make our sorrow their life-spring to turn
'Gainst death another answer. But the pain
Will be so great, the fiery jaws of fate
Will close so quick upon them, they shall fail.
Another nothingness will haunt their slime,
Their monstrous cities, battered by the gale,
Shall go down too. Death in some secret shape

Shall come upon them. God's great Serpent still
That parts us from our hopes here will prevail
Across the skies to mock their final dream:
Darkness will take them and an unending stream
Of tears and woes and hopes will sweep their world away.

PART SEVEN

THE PRELUDE OF STORM

From the midsummer's rushing flood,
From the storm on the horizon crouched and hiding,
Blue-black bellied clouds surging onwards through heat with
    flickerings of fierce desire,
From the joy too swift and sudden to be quickly understood,
The strong whiplash of the autumn wind out of the north-
    east riding,
To summon with his crackling lightning-whip this torrent of
    blazing fire,
Let there come at last our peace, and a silent hope of abiding.

From the summit between the onracing cloud and the sun,
Lashed with the rattling bullets of hail rending to ribbons
    the wind-fluttered leaves,
From the hour after noon when the sun
Scatters the silver-grey cloud-rack and the dreamy peace of
    the autumn succeeds,
From the crimson flakes uncooled to ash in the roar of the
    central flame,
The gods having long since descended, their secret ours ever
    to keep,
We move through the slow dance of time, forever now vary-
    ing, yet ever the same,

Immortal in mortal transcended, till, weary, we turn then
and sleep.

SONG OF THE MIDNIGHT RAIN

There was rain without, and lightning stalked into the room;
But, in our hearts, there was joy that transcended all pain;
The gloom of the midnight grew dense, but through thick
    strands of rain,
We arose as on tense wings of angels over our gloom.

There was song in the night and the thought of you there
    at my side,
Filling my heart with fresh glory, till it forgot every wrong;
The tide of our love rose and fell and its pull was so strong,
That its beauty in us could ever swell and abide.

There was dawn at the last, and the chalice of love drained
    deep,
The clouds through the morning passing, the curtain of close
    night withdrawn.
Outstretched in white beauty you lay at the coming forth
    of the day;
We had wandered all night in the garden, hid behind ram-
    parts of sleep.

PROMENADE BY THE AUTUMN RIVER

Beside the ancient river, where three cypresses had stood
Above the sluggish current, under a slate-grey sky,
Storm ravelling over the zenith, as in a dream, the mood
Of quiet deep upon me, we wandered by and by.

Strong weariness was in my heart of worlds I could not win,
Old hopes by fortune thwarted, grim battles long since past;
Here was the flame of summer fading, and winter drawing
    in;
My weary head upon your lap lay quiet at the last.

Perhaps the river whispered of the children there at play,
The boys gone nutting in the woods, the girls who scurried
    round
The tethered houseboats in the stream—perhaps the flood
    could say
If there would come new years for me where hopes might
    yet abound.

Slate-grey and still and sullen the river slipped to south;
Beside it, ranks of knotted seines, stretched out on stakes and
    poles.
Even in my desolation I know it is your mouth
That holds for me the future and the best of this life's goals.

Summer now ebbs and song
Ebbs with the summer; yet
There may be days erelong
To make our hearts forget

How near the winter lags,
How closely comes the frost,
As scarlet sumach flags
The swamp,—as, lonely, lost,

The solemn cypress burns
Its russet towers in the sky;
As the wild goose returns,
And the wild flowers die.

Here Indian summer made—
A runner stilled in flight—
One day with love arrayed,
A day that knew no night.

We sat in a hauled-up boat,
The river flashed like stone.
Your throat against my throat,
Four eyes that looked as one.

Four hands that intertwined;
Your head against my head;
The hours ran undesigned,
What was it that you said?

What was the hope that hid
Here where no hope could fill
My cup that to the lid
Stood brimming? What the will?

Ask Indian summer, now
Sped on to southward fast;
Or ask him not, but vow
This love was given to last;

Ask autumn sumach still
Scarlet on dove-grey sky;
Or ask it not, but will
This love shall never die.

THE GIFTS DEMANDED

Give me four walls,
And I will make them paradise;
They shall shine ever in my eyes
For you.

Give me two chairs,
And they will be two thrones;
More than the mightiest monarch owns,
With you.

Give me a cup of wine,
And I will drink it to the final lees,

Knowing love's ease
Through you.

Give me the world,
Poor, pitiful, stupid world;
Like a gold flag I bear unfurled
Through it my love for you.

TO AN AUTUMN ROSE

That rose you gave me, sweetheart, at the last,
Soft orange, exquisite in the warm autumn air,
When azure skies watch blue-black clouds run fast;
That rose, beloved, still is blooming there.

That lovely rose beside my bed blooms on,
Full-petalled, drooping through our parting night;
And will awake beside me as the dawn
Comes to my window, bids the dusk take flight.

Token it was of that exultant force,
That rose, which brought back Eden on earth again;
Soft orange tinged with pink; now no remorse
Or evil spell could ever make us twain.

Since we are one, beloved, one in joy
And one in hope; since now no barrier stands
Between us; since as smiling girl and boy,
We wandered where the rose-tree lights all lands.

THE VOW

By the vow of the earth and the cloud,
You shall be mine:

By the great oaks unbowed,
By winter's sleeping shroud;
By the might of love endowed,
You shall be mine.

By the hawberries, crimson,
Deep in the sombre russet of the swamp;
By the sun striking its last shafts amid them,
Kindling their boughs to unimagined pomp;

You shall be mine,
As the sun to south, away,
Comes northward once again
Spreading afar new day.

CONVERSATION WITH A MIDWINTER SKY

As I went home on that midwinter night,
Fresh from the banquet of joy that you had spread me there,
I saw against the steel-blue zenith, glittering, bright,
The host of the winter stars in that keen frosty air.

Orion stood far south; great Sirius blazed
With bright green bale-fire; high, the Pleiades

Hung their faint cluster; and the Swan upraised
Her wings as breasting down the northeast breeze.

These spoke to me in their strange, twinkling speech
Which was ere the Chaldean shepherds, long ago,
Watched them from waste plateaus and named them each,
Winter and summer rising and setting so:

"We wanderers of the vast in which you stand,
Mote-midget on your tiny speck of space,
By our light-beams the infinite have spanned
Myriads of ages ere the human race.

"We wheel and veer and turn at time's dark bidding,
Herd of the heaven's void, who move from far to far;
While you return to that familiar dwelling
Made hallowed by the race-hopes which you are.

"Not any instant of the enormous span,
Nor any beam from out proud galaxies,
Could match the light within you, son of man,
Since you have found it where no triumph dies;

"In love full-shared and offered; keen as air,
As fire enkindling, and as oceans deep;
As earth made perfect for exploring there.
We wander here unsated; you may sleep."

DREAM OF THE RED ROSE

This is the dream I had before the dawn,
The night you, sweetheart, gave the red rose to me;
Whose perfume, from its silken petals free,
Hung over my pillow till the night was gone.

I thought that we two fled
Down moss-hung woodlands of an older South
Harried with war; we had been driven forth
That morning by the Federal guns which came
Jostling down red clay roads, past cabins barred,
To shell the town; behind us now came roars;
Explosions of loud shells, swift spurts of flame,
Mad shots and yells; before us open stood
Dim woodlands with their valleys running south,
Hung with grey moss: the marsh, the plain, the sea,
The unknown world.

                    Love, we have come
Where opens now before us like a sea
Circling to sunset, this new life; its waves
Are tinged with gold at sunset, blue at dawn,
Running forever varied, ever free,
Towards the future shore where we will be
One with great lovers of the years bygone;
With Paris and with Helen, Tristan, Faust,
With Guinevere and Launcelot, Ming-Huang,
Yang Kuei-fei, Radha and Krishna, and
With Isis and Osiris.

Wrapped in grey winter's shroud,
Love, with its steady flame, mocks still at frost;
Love seeks completion, love awaits the spring,
Love comes unbidden, love is welcome guest;
At every meeting love is in our hearts,
Forever varying, ever yet the same.

This is the dream I had before the dawn,
The night you, sweetheart, gave the red rose to me;
Whose perfume, from its silken petals free,
Hangs over my heart now, till this song be gone.

TO A FACE IN THE FIRELIGHT

Are you reality, or are you dream,
You with the soft warm lamplight playing on face and hair;
You with the dove-grey eyes, the delicate hands,
Sitting beside me there?

Are you reality, or are you dream?
Something I merely hoped for, or rich and tender dust;
I scarcely dare to stir and touch you, dear:
And yet love says I must.

Are you reality or are you dream?
Without the carols are crying that Christ is born;
Where the world, darkened by new doom of war,
Moves to this Christmas morn.

[228]

I dare not guess if you are real or no.
If you are real, it is only for my sake;
And if a dream, may that dream go on so
I shall not need to wake.

SYMPHONY OF THE NEW YEAR

I

Year's end and dream's end and life's proud awakening
After the flight through storms, the song of love's raging
    torrent,
Flying like floods from the mountains, onrush of mad des-
    perate water
Leaping through long hills of granite, overflowing the
    cypress-filled plains;
Year's end and dream's end, and life moving steadily on-
    wards,
Flood in great force now unleashed with lightnings and dark
    cloud above it;
We two caught on a frail tiny skiff, carried onward and south-
    ward before it;
Clasped in each other's arms, having found now the love
    that will last out our day.

We two hearts apart, dissatisfied, brought by God together;
To us love comes unexpected, a vast power tirelessly de-
    scending

In glimmer of firelight, in white snow that whirls through
    the streets,
In hawberries' scarlet clusters when the leaves are gone;
In sumach's startling flare, in wine-red dogwood;
In summer's change to fall, in the slow hush of heat
When wan moon silver washes fields with mist,
After the sun's slow brassy march through day has gone,
Low flimsy scarves that sweep athwart black trees
That lead to unforgotten changeless dawn.

Grief's end and loneliness' end and life still uprising
With our two hearts united, eager and keen to meet it;
Parting's end and storm's end and the sun's resurrection-
    coming
Up from the Gulf, new washed, reborn, to shine in level
    lands;
To fill the hills with the song of the birds and the snow-
    flake flower of the dogwood,
To set men striving at their tasks, to bid ploughs furrow the
    earth;
To kindle in our own two hearts the love without change or
    failing,
The love in which the gods themselves, through our flesh,
    find their way.

II

The pines cover densely the mountain;
They hold up their fine-needled branches
Huge in the heat and unhurried,

[230]

From ridge behind ridge, high and secret,
The pines look over the land.

From South Fourche to Forkéd Mountain,
Dense and dull green and unchanging,
Unhewn by an axe, stand the pines;
Under the curtain of heat.

I am your pine;
Sheltering densely the dark earth below me;
You came in the evening, stood near me;
You touched with your soft hands my bark.
Now love, like a thundercloud surging,
Through azure skies rolling and coiling,
Has cast down my cones and my needles,
And strewn them all there at your feet.

III

Lonely I waited, hoping for the love
That would fulfil my heart; the night was long,
Hour after hour ticked off to sombre darkness.
Alone and hoping only that at dawn
You would send word, I lay; for in my heart,
Unchanging, steady, love kept perfect tune,
But you were not there to answer; far away
You stayed and maybe did not think of me, to whom
A few brief hours ago, there came such love
As made all other joys on earth grow pale,
Such song as seemed my dream; where was it now?

[231]

Where was the hope my love had so heaped up
About you ere you fled? Now utterly gone,
There was nothing left for me but to wake and pray.

So nights of parting went; but in this year,
There is no parting now; unless the pain
I gave you, dearest, with my blundering thought,
My rude, plain, honest love should hurt you so
You could not bear it; then indeed a darkness
Greater than any suffered in my life,
Would take me utterly, and I be lost,
With only the memory how much I failed
To cherish you, to win and keep you mine,
Still torturing me—if you are not happy now.

IV

They lay together quickened, all that night;
Safe in the arms of God, all through the night:
They shared each other's sleep, the livelong night;
They joyed in each other's presence, deep in night.
They knew love bright and perfect, for one night;
Breast set to shining breast; long, long the night;
They were not weary nor sated, nor did night
Afright them; glorious, perfect was the night.
There came between a bond, forged deep from night,
As joy made pure and perfect, 'spite of night;
These two storm-tested souls who had known the night,
Accepted and transcended so the night.

[232]

V

As the guests went home,
I saw, against the moonlight on the lawn,
Etched black and vast and motionless, at peace,
The great magnolia's gloom.

It is eternal, like my love for you;
Love like none other, shaped of tenderness
Blossoming and fruiting, filled with bright red seeds,
With fiery passion sleeping at its core.

A century long the vast magnolia holds
Its strength unaltering up against the sky.
But in my heart I find
Each day my love for you reborn anew.

Fill now my soul with that vast silence shaped
Of multitudinous leaves;
Make every one of them green, shining, great,
Each one an image of the years bygone,
Each one a promise of swift-coming spring.

THE WEDDING RING

Delicately chased, rare metal, pale as ice,
Engraved without with many a quaint device
Of orange blossom, now this fairy ring
I give to you, my dear, as my sole offering.

It is the first and it shall be the last
Of wedding rings I give; and may it hold us fast;
Body and soul commingled, till your heart
Dissolves with mine in earth's last peace apart.

In my own month of birth I gave it; now
As symbol of rebirth, it serves to show
How love requickened walks and leaps and flies,
Through us and in us, ever in sweet surprise.

So much it holds of new-made blossoming;
Midwinter's flame of hope; fair journeys in the spring;
Heaven to earth brought close through days and nights
Of toil and joy; sunset beyond the heights.

Laughter and gipsying and a living place
In memory; a road I would retrace;
And shall, perhaps, in life-blood of a son.
All this is in my ring which makes us one.

Delicately chased, rare metal, grey as ice,
Engraved within with our names—quaint device—
This ring I pledge you, pledging so my soul
Forever and ever, long as the world may roll.

AT THE OLD HOUSE

Facing the ancient house,
Shuttered and silent, we, through the soft March day,
Wandered, hand clasped in hand,

[234]

Amid the daffodils, which kindled their array
'Gainst the grape-hyacinths glowing,
Deep azure darkening their hearts to midnight blue.
Facing the ancient house, we two,
As a ritual of farewell to this our land,
Went, on each other love and joy bestowing;
While the fresh breeze from the south blew up our way.
The old house emptily drowsed;
Dark cedars watched, quite still;
Long piny hills stood lank, as lacking will
The vacant land to rouse
Until it saw us go;
We in whose hearts love kept its perfect glow
Like to the redbud, deep
Rose blent with violet, moved against the sleep
Of the old walls where pure gold trumpets, slow,
Blew up for spring their challenge. And I know
There by the ancient house,
With all its doors and windows silent set,
Such love to me in riotous power was given
As Dante might have felt for Beatrice, had they met
Somewhere at last on earth, and not remote in heaven.

ASCENT OF MONADNOCK

I

Deep through the midcourse of morning
Is shadowed the base of the mountain;

Under the wings of the stormcloud,
Only the top peak takes light.

I would climb up against shadow,
Leaving the lost past behind me;
I would move up through the darkness,
Breasting each crag till it pass.

I would come out where the rocks
Glow, shadeless granite beneath the broad sun,
Till my soul on the summit, set free there,
Breathes naked air, and pure light.

II

The mountain stands aloof:
Blue-black its bulk upshouldered on the sky:
Its brooding power made vast
In memory's afternoon.

Now summer drifts away,
That flung green leaves far upward to its base;
The feathery alleys of the fern and spruce
Are lit with goldenrod in drooping sprays.

In heart I climbed,
While my eyes measured heights I dared not scale;
In heart I kept
Faith that beyond the darkness there was light.

[236]

Let shadow stay,
And make remote this final peak of life;
Till on the last steep crags
There spreads the pure cloak of the cloud's snow-white.

III

Up the grim slopes we went
Toilsomely, foot by foot;
Love flowering in two lives,
As from a single root:

Up granites never changed
To greet the changing sky;
And saw, by wood and pond,
The clouds float lazily by.

You for whom, had I power,
I'd give this glittering world;
And I on whom, each hour,
Love rose again and stirred;

We two trod the last slopes,
Laughter and light and peace;
And sat down on the stones,
And saw the sky's increase:

Each field and tree and farm
Of which we formed a part;
Love had not lost its aim
Since you lived in my heart.

[237]